101SEX

Things You Didn't Know about

EVE MARX

Avon, Massachusetts

For

Buttons,

true of heart

Copyright © 2009 by F+W Media, Inc.
All rights reserved.
This book, or parts thereof, may not be reproduced in any
form without permission from the publisher; exceptions are
made for brief excerpts used in published reviews.

Published by
Adams Media, a division of F+W Media, Inc.
57 Littlefield Street, Avon, MA 02322. U.S.A.
www.adamsmedia.com

ISBN 10: 1-60550-106-9
ISBN 13: 978-1-60550-106-2

Printed in the United States of America.

J I H G F E D C B A

Library of Congress Cataloging-in-Publication Data
is available from the publisher.

Interior images © 2009 Jupiterimages Corporation

*This book is available at quantity discounts for bulk purchases.
For information, please call 1-800-289-0963.*

Acknowledgments

First and foremost, I'd like to thank Nevine Michaan, yoga guru, café owner, friend, chocolate lover, and swami. Nevine gave me a gorgeous handmade cloth paper journal I admired that she sells in her unique shop, Bhoomi Café, in Bedford Hills, New York, and that's how the book got started.

A warm thanks to Lynn Biederman, friend and author of the brilliant young adult novel, *Unraveling*, who took to heart my call for questions. I guess everybody else I asked must have been too embarrassed! Although I suspect Lynn knows just about everything there is to know about sex (and there is a surprising amount of sex in her novel), she still managed to come up with good questions.

A special thanks to my friend Mitch Horn, documentary filmmaker, lover of gay rodeo, and general bon vivant, for providing me with encouragement and entertainment during the long writing process. Thank you Ruth James for reading the book in bits and pieces. Also on my list to thank are my amazing riding partners, Janet and Hayley, whom I met at the barn, at Buxton Pond Farm, where we keep our horses. For months as I worked on the book, as we were grooming and picking out feet and tacking up, these lovely ladies put up with (or turned a deaf ear to) my constant chatter about things I was putting in the book before we set out on our trail rides. And speaking of horses, I owe my most particular thanks my own darling pony, Buttons, for his courage, his enthusiasm, his steadiness, and his willingness to carry me anywhere.

My family deserves a great big hug for their love and support and patience. R.J. and Sam, you rock. And a big thank you goes to my agent, the unflappable June Clark, as well as to the folks at Adams Media, editors Paula Munier and Wendy Simard, and designers Elisabeth Lariviere and Denise Wallace, for their hard work on the book.

Contents

Introduction

For as long as I can remember, I've been curious about sex. Not just the act, or acts, or even personally having sex (although I have to say, I've had quite a lot), but simply about all things sexual. It could be that I was just a preternaturally sexually curious child, but from a young age, I was captivated by images and impressions relating to sex.

That I was able to turn my deep and abiding interest into a bonafide career still sometimes surprises me! My interest in sex is partly academic, partly anthropological, partly voyeuristic. It is both a blessing and a curse that people—even near strangers!—want to tell me about their sex lives!

There's a great deal of hue and cry right now about how sex is the only thing that sells and how there is too much emphasis on sex in modern culture. And it's true, we sit through a lot of lousy movies just because we heard it's got a steamy sex scene, and we're far more likely to pick up a book to read if we know it's got a sexy passage. Sex appeal is a principal reason why we buy cars, clothes, jewelry, undergo pricey cosmetic procedures, take exotic vacations, and travel around the world, motivated, many times, simply by the possibility of sex. Sex, like food and drink, is one of the great driving forces. No wonder we're all obsessed by it!

101 Things You Didn't Know about Sex is meant to be an informative, hip, modern, and unabashedly nonclinical look at sex, offering the kind of juicy bits not usually taught in health class—unless you just happened to be in attendance at an extremely progressive and open-minded classroom. All the material covered in this crash course on human sexuality and behavior is true, but far from what you'd learn from your mom—unless your mom is Dr. Ruth. In these pages you will find useful and pertinent information on everything from birth control to sexual preferences to how to arrange a threesome. While not exactly encyclopedic in scope, I've tried to provide a sizeable span of sexual topics to inform *and* entertain.

1

You have almost no control over what or whom you find sexy.

Instant attraction, love at first sight, the power of scent, slow-burn love, how opposites attract, are all part and parcel of what we call "sex appeal." Instantaneous sex appeal and how we connect with another person mostly has to do with physical and psychological factors we may have little or no control over.

Instant attraction, it turns out, is almost always based on early presexual and sensual experiences. For example, remember the first person you had a big crush on? His or her type will always be a trigger for you, ingrained forever into your most basic sensory system.

Your culture also plays a big part in who you find sexy. For example, because American culture is so fascinated with large breasts, many males born and raised here are programmed from an early age to respond to women with large breasts. Movies, television, style and trend

PILLOW *talk*

Love
is a matter of
chemistry,
but
sex
is a matter of
physics.

—Unknown

magazines, in fact the entire cult of celebrity, informs our thinking as to who we think is sexy, and most of us happily accept their decree.

Sex appeal stemming from the rules of "opposites attract," grows out of an unconscious desire to be with someone who has something that we lack. That's one of the reasons why an introvert can be attracted to an extrovert!

Then there's mirroring, which means we like people who look or smell a lot like ourselves. That's the reason why so many redheads adore other redheads, and blonds go for other blonds!

Slow-burn sex appeal develops when you discover that feelings you have for the person you've been hanging out with all the time as a friend suddenly turn erotic. The attraction and the sex appeal develop when you realize how much you have in common. Attraction to another person is also triggered by dopamine in the brain that tells you that you're liking what you're seeing and now you want more of it.

Pheromones, that is, the natural scent exuding from your body, play a big part in sex appeal, but don't expect to have any control over them. Pricey perfumes and colognes may initially boost your sex appeal to the object of your desire, but at the end of the day, if he or she can't deal with your sweat, the relationship isn't going anywhere!

Whether oral sex is actually *sex* depends on whom you ask.

The jury's out on this one. And there may be an age-related bias. A lot of young men and women don't think of oral sex as real sex or at least not serious sex. Certainly former president Bill Clinton said it was not. Besides men of stature, many people disagree on whether oral sex counts as sex or not. A large number of people in America at least think that sex acts that include penile/vaginal penetration or penile/anal penetration are bonafide sex, while anything else, and that would include finger action, frottage (a French lesbian move involving lots of pelvic rubbing and grinding), and oral sex is just playin'. Foolin' around. Puppy love? On the other hand, ask any woman whose husband has dallied outside the marriage on the receiving end of a blow job if she thinks he cheated on her and the answer is yes. Ask a guy the same question and he'll probably say no. Maybe it's a gender bias?

PILLOW *talk*

I happen to like *uncomplicated* sex.

—Sigourney Weaver

no.
3

It's been said that an orgasm is similar to a sneeze.

The build-up, the anticipation, the release . . . those are three reasons why orgasms are frequently compared to a sneeze. Kind of a diminishing way to view orgasms, though, isn't it? There is a legend that having eight sneezes in a row will produce an orgasm and another that ten sneezes in a row is the equivalent of an orgasm. Like an orgasm, a sneeze is an unrestrained physical response. In the case of a sneeze, it's triggered by the body's perception that something has to be expelled from the nose. But sneezing, unlike orgasm, can also be set off in some people by exposure to a lot of bright light (this is known as photogenic sneezing), or even by combing one's hair too hard! Sneezing also causes temporary incontinence, which is why some women pee a little when they sneeze. The liquid produced from an orgasm, whether it's semen or female ejaculate, is definitely not pee, however!

Pillow *talk*

Winning is like sex, the more you do it, the more you *like* it.

–Felix Sabates

no.
4

Same-sex dalliances are fairly common among teen and twenty-something girls; less so among adult women.

If you're fooling around in bed with your same sex best friend and wondering if you might be a lesbian, there are some things to consider first. When you're a young female adolescent your hormones are raging and you're in a continually aroused state, a lot of things seem possible, including having sex with a buddy or a wild same-sex hookup with a total stranger. Does it mean that you're a lesbian? Nah. This goes for guys too, but only really young ones. Most guys are sexually mature by the age of eighteen. They know by then whether they go for guys or for girls. Unless they're bi, and then they enjoy both, although even among bisexuals, there's usually a preference.

You can swap spit, fool around, get naked, share a hot tub, have sex with a person the same sex as you—and not be gay. You can even be in a long-term, same-sex sexual relationship and still not be a homo. How come? Because sexual orientation is something that must be declared. You have to say you're gay to be gay or you're not gay or you're ambivalent. Consider the woman who told another woman at a party that she had just come off a twelve-year relationship with another woman. "So you're gay?" her new friend said. "No, I'm not gay," the woman said. "I was in a gay relationship."

Chances are you're gay if you find yourself exclusively drawn to and aroused by persons of the same gender. Another indicator that you're really gay is if you never experience physical or romantic attraction or desire to any person of the opposite sex. Or it's possible that you don't know what you are because you still haven't met the right person. And since there is still no identifiable gene that denotes sexuality, there's no medical way to test for gender preference. Yet.

PILLOW
talk

Sex is part of
nature. I go along
with nature.

—Marilyn Monroe

no.
5

With sex, you can get better with age!

While it's true that younger people have the physical advantage of being more athletic, having more stamina, and being physically more flexible. Younger people also possess more of those raging hormones that propel people into having sex. The downside for young people is that they can also be more inhibited and fearful about sex. Young people are also more concerned with how they look naked. They also tend to be less communicative with each other while they're having sex. They are also less open to experimentation or exploring sexual fetishes.

Now for the advantages older has over younger. Older women, particularly the oft-described 'cougar,' that is a woman who is at least in her late thirties, are more capable of experiencing multiple orgasms than younger women. These older ladies also feel more free with their bodies, and are are less inhibited about trying new things, like sex toys

PILLOW *talk*

Sex appeal

*is fifty percent
what you've
got and fifty
percent what
people*
think
you've got.

—Sophia Loren

or new positions or engaging in role play. And while it's true that older guys are slower to become hard and even slower to ejaculate, this often makes them better, more tender lovers because they will take the time and have the willingness to engage in extended foreplay. Because women benefit from prolonged foreplay (the longer the build-up, the more intense the female orgasm), it's easy to understand why many women of all ages, prefer an older guy. Older men are willing to take their time with a woman, while young studs are all about speed and vigor!

A true bisexual does not discriminate between the sexes for partners.

A bisexual is a person who is sexually attracted to men and women, although usually one more than the other. A female bisexual can desire male and female partners, and a male bisexual will do the same. Someone who is truly bisexual doesn't discriminate between the sexes. They will have sex with whomever they are attracted to at that particular moment, regardless of gender.

The majority of people who are bisexual, however, never or rarely act at all on their desires. This is mostly because of strong societal taboos against folks who pitch for both teams. It's also why many closeted bisexuals sublimate their attraction to people they desire. Lots of women who are married to men are sexually attracted to other women whom they will never kiss or sleep with. And because lesbian culture openly frowns on women who shuttle back and forth between hetero and homo lifestyles, many women in committed relationships with other women pleasure themselves fantasizing about sex with men! There are openly gay men who fancy and have sex on occasion with women, just as there are married men who are sexually attracted to other men, relationships they cultivate as friends . . . and not "friends with benefits," either! Many people who consider themselves to be strictly hetero are surprised to discover that the real reason they're drawn to a particular person of their own gender is because they subconsciously want to hump him or her! The subconscious is amazing! Many bisexual relationships are not so much sexual as they are romantic. This is the real story behind so many male and female BFFs.

Bisexuals are not necessarily equally attracted to men and women. They usually favor one gender over the other. Is it possible to be just a little bit bisexual? Yes, said sexual researcher Alfred Kinsey, fifty years ago, when he scrutinized human sexual behavior. At the time, Kinsey created a seven-point scale for the purpose of evaluating sexual orientation. According to how you answered Kinsey's questions, you could be labeled, "exclusively hetero," "exclusively homo," or just "incidentally homosexual," easy enough to imagine if you suddenly find yourself doing a long stint in prison! Although his methodology was roundly attacked and criticized, Kinsey's scale is still in use to help define the ambiguities of bisexuality.

A phenomenon of "bisexual chic," took place in the 1980s when cult-classic films like *My Own Private Idaho*, and *Basic Instinct* hit the screens and when stars like R.E.M.'s Michael Stipe alluded to their own bisexual tendencies. Celebrity bisexuals include David Bowie, Dave Navarro, Anne Heche, and Cynthia Nixon.

PILLOW *talk*

Sexual love is the most stupendous fact of the universe, and the most magical mystery our poor blind senses know.

—Amy Lowell

Pheromones can lead you to your ideal lover.

Biologists describe pheromones as "smellprints" that supposedly are as unique to each person as his or her fingerprint. Smell is the most primitive of human senses and, unlike sight and touch, smell travels a direct route to the brain's limbic lobe where it can provoke an emotional reaction that can be, quite literally, a turn-on.

The first pheromone ever identified was in 1956 when a team of German researchers discovered that certain glands that could be removed from the abdomen of female moths had an extraordinary effect on male moths who, after being exposed to it, beat their little wings off in a fluttering mating dance. Sea urchins, it was soon after discovered, release pheromones into surrounding water to send a chemical message triggering other urchins in the colony to simultaneously eject their sex cells. Human sexuality and pheromones became connected in 1986, when Dr.

Winifred Cutler, a biologist and behavioral endocrinologist, discovered pheromones in our underarms. She and her team of researchers published a scientific article proving that after overbearing nasty underarm sweat was removed, what was left behind were odorless materials containing pheromones. Dr. Cutler went on to create and market a commercially developed pheromone she called Athena, which women could topically apply to attract men. Seventy-four percent of the women who tested the product reported an increase in hugging, kissing, and sexual intercourse. Hey, this stuff really works!

Today it is recognized that pheromones can be used as fertility treatments for couples who want to conceive, or as contraceptives for those who don't. Couples who are experiencing sexual problems can use pheromones combined with traditional therapy to amplify desire. Many researchers believe it's possible that pheromones will one day be used to alleviate depression, help us deal with stress, and enhance our mood. *(Goodbye Zoloft, hello, pheromones?!)* It is believed that one day pheromone treatment therapies may control prostate activity in men to reduce their risk of cancer.

One thing that is known for sure is that pheromones in your body scent are the main reason why we're attracted to one person and not another. An article published in *Psychology Today* explained how body odors that are perceived as pleasant and sexy to one person are a total turn-off to someone else. Sexual attraction, it turns out, is a highly

PILLOW talk

selective process and to some degree, something that humans (or insects or even sea urchins) have little control over. We can't help it: our biology is set up so that we smell the best to the person whose genetically based immunity to disease differs most from our own. This benefits us all in the long run, because it makes for healthier and genetically stronger offspring.

Really, sex and laughter do go very well together, and I wondered— and I still do—which is more important.

—Hermione Gingold

18

no.

8

Aside from the G spot, there's an A spot, and a U spot!

The G spot, also called the Grafenberg spot for German gynecologist Dr. Ernst Grafenberg who in 1944 claimed to have discovered it, is a female erogenous zone. When stimulated, the G spot is said to produce high levels of sexual arousal and mind-blowing, even ejaculatory, female orgasms.

The G spot is thought to be located directly behind the pubic bone surrounding the urethra, accessible through the anterior or front wall of the vagina. Sometimes likened to an accessory clitoris, the G spot is thought to be best stimulated by deep massage of the mons veneris or by using a feminine massage tool specially designed to reach up and under the pubic bone. Both the G spot and the clitoris are believed to share a common nerve and the stimulation of one is described as often stimulating the other.

PILLOW
talk

Sex
is a
discovery.

—Fannie Hurst

Whether or not the G spot actually exists remains an open question in the medical and scientific community; however, many if not most women believe it is real. Popular sexology books take its existence for granted. The G spot may actually be the Skenes gland, sometimes called the female prostate. The Skenes gland is a system of glands and ducts surrounding the urethra. It has been scientifically proven to be connected to female ejaculation of a fluid that is not urine. The Skenes gland system is located within the anterior (front wall) of the vagina, in about the same place the G spot is reckoned to exist.

New information about the G spot, whose existence has remained controversial since the 1980s, recently surfaced when BBC News reported that an Italian scientist named Dr. Emmanuele Jannini of the University of L'Aquila announced that the mysterious G spot can be found with ultrasound. Dr. Jannini told *New Scientist* magazine about an area of thicker tissue in the region believed to be the G spot that had been discovered among women reporting orgasms. Ultrasound was then used to document and measure the size and shape of this tissue beyond the front wall of the vagina, which is often suggested as the location of the G spot area.

Sexual aids and devices and toys specifically designed to massage the G spot proliferate across the Internet, and the high volume of sales for such items suggests that many women wish to be more in touch with theirs. Buyers beware before placing an order for your own Natural

Contours Ultime G spot massager priced at $39.95, although approval ratings for this product remain high. Sensitivity does vary from woman to woman.

The "A-Spot," (or the Anterior Fornix Erogenous Zone) is a newly discovered patch of sensitive tissue at the deepest point of the front wall of the vagina between the cervix and the bladder. Direct stimulation of this spot can produce delicious, multiple orgasmic contractions.

The "U-Spot" (or Skene's gland) is a small patch of sensitive erectile tissue located on the front wall of the vagina, around the lower end of the urethra. Sometimes referred to as the "female prostate," but less well known than the clitoris, its erotic potential was only recently investigated by American clinical research workers. They found that if this region was gently caressed, with the finger, the tongue, or the tip of the penis, it could produce an unexpectedly powerful response. Some even believe that female ejaculation is related to the Skene's gland!

All women can learn how to deep throat.

Deep throat is, in a nutshell, advanced fellatio. It's all about how far you can get that guy's equipment down your throat. What's required in deep throat, which has to be learned and then practiced, is an ability to override the body's natural gag reflex.

To successfully perform deep throat, his penis has to get behind her tonsils, which is where the gag reflex begins. Assuming you still have tonsils, that is. Repeatedly swallowing during fellatio keeps the saliva flowing, making it easier for the penis to glide further down the throat. Repeated swallowing also keeps air moving, which helps override the gag reflex. Professional sword swallowers master these techniques, which not so coincidentally makes them great deep throaters. Many women enjoy performing fellatio and excel at it, thereby gaining great confidence for having mastered this ancient sexual art.

PILLOW *talk*

In my sex fantasy,
nobody ever loves
me for my *mind*.

–Nora Ephron

The "bible of love" details hundreds of ways to do it.

This sacred book—otherwise known as the Kama Sutra—dates back to ancient India. For example, it lists and details eight different forms of love biting that range from a slight reddening of the skin to significant wounding. Dozens of positions are described, including positions of "high congress," which are meant to widen a less experienced woman's vulva for the male's most promising access. Each of these positions has a name, such as the "The Wife of Indra," which describes a woman lying flat on her back with her knees drawn to her chest. Clasping position, the pressing position, the twinning position, or the mare's position, may be chosen because they make an older (and more stretched out) woman's vagina seem tighter and smaller. Sexual positions are named for animals, such as the cat's position, the spider position, the elephant position, or the jump of the hare.

PILLOW *talk*

The true feeling of sex is that of a deep **intimacy**, *but above all of a deep* **complicity**.

—James Dickey

Intercourse in which the inner lips of the vagina only experience friction, but not entering force, by the penis is broken down into many levels of intimacy ranging from teasing and tickling to the more forceful smacking of the head of the penis against the female labia, an act called in the Kama Sutra "blow of the boar." Even if you've never seen this amazing and dynamic book, know that there are dozens and dozens and dozens of ways to have sex. It could take an entire lifetime to try them all out!

Female ejaculate was a topic Aristotle wrote about thousands of years ago.

So how come nobody still really is sure what it is? Great minds have pondered the mystery of female ejaculation since B.C., but the jury is still out. A great many modern sexperts and researchers claim such a thing exists, while others stick with the camp that says female ejaculate is just a case of excessive lubrication—or urine. Anecdotal evidence suggests that many women do have the ability to squirt. For example, anyone can watch women squirting away on YouTube. It's easy to see: check it out! But precisely what these ladies are squirting is scientifically unclear.

Most of the clinical discussions on the subject revolve around the female prostate and the G spot. (More on the G spot in #8). Gushers, as these ladies are called, produce a small amount of clear fluid that contains only trace amounts of uric acid. The fluid doesn't look like urine,

PILLOW *talk*

The sexual **embrace** *can only be compared with* **music** *and with* **prayer**.

—Marcus Aurelius

doesn't smell like urine, and in laboratory tests with chemical analyses, what they have produced is indeed not urine. Taste it and it's almost sweet. The fluid itself comes from the paraurethral ducts during orgasm. Sex researchers think it comes from the Skenes gland. While many men and certainly a lot of lesbians find the idea of female ejaculate pretty sexy, many women are embarrassed by it. Some think it is incontinence (i.e., pissing the bed).

Until the 1980s, female ejaculate was more or less ignored by the medical community, although it has been a subject in anatomical, biological, and medical literature since classical antiquity. Back around 325 B.C., probably around the time he was accused of impiety, Aristotle wrote about it, and in the second century, the Roman physician Galen described it. During the Italian Renaissance, Renaldus Columbus, an anatomist, wrote about female ejaculate in his explanation of the clitoris. Much more recently, the sex researchers John Perry and Beverly Whipple studied large groups of women who were able to produce ejaculate and determined it to be an alkaline substance secreted by the paraurethral ducts and glands, also called Skene's gland. They said that the gland also produces Human Protein 1, a characteristic formerly believed to be unique to the male prostate. Squirts emerge only after intense stimulation to the front of the vaginal wall and not simply through stimulation of the clitoris. The holistic take on all this is that female ejaculate is not a myth, it's not urine, and that any woman can produce it. All it takes is getting past your inhibitions, a good how-to tape, and to cut loose with the juice.

12

Vaseline plus condoms don't mix.

Vaseline, America's favorite greasy rub, spells disaster when used as a sexual lubricant! That's because Vaseline is a petroleum product and petroleum destroys latex. By destroy, we mean eats. In a matter of minutes, Vaseline on a condom or a diaphragm will make a hole! Repeat after me: Never use Vaseline! The fact is, no oil-based product should ever be used in conjunction with a diaphragm or a condom. That means no Vaseline, no baby oil, no hand lotion. These products are all recognized to create pinholes in latex, which could lead to the exchange of an STD or accidental pregnancy. Not exactly what you hand in mind when you set out to have a good time.

When you're thinking protection, what you should be using as a personal lubricant to get past the pinch of rubber is KY jelly, or the generic KY-type lubricant also sold in every American drugstore. The warming

KY, which is a relatively new product, is really nice and has the added benefit of removing that clammy "yuck," feeling when you apply it. Petroleum products are now also on every environmentalist's no-no list, so you'll be doing the planet a favor by dumping them out of your medicine cabinet. Be safe and go green at the same time!

PILLOW *talk*

How
love
the
limb-loosener
sweeps
me away.

—Sappho

That sexy glow is real!

Guess what? It's not a rash! A post-sex glow is quite literally the flush on a woman's skin, causing it to turn pink. This glow is the end result of increased blood flow to the surface of the body. The glow occurs in approximately 50 percent of women, and is more common in women with fair skin. For some women, it's also definitely affected by warmer weather. The flush, which sometimes looks like spots, can appear on the face, the neck, the breasts, and the belly. How long does it last? Usually it recedes and then entirely goes away within a half hour to forty-five minutes. Pssst: Men are particularly aware of it when a woman has the "glow."

Is it possible to keep that glow going by using heightened senses? For that specific glow, no, because it's purely physiological. Good sex after all is aerobic. But there are other kinds of glows. For example you can get yourself wet again just by reliving in your imagination a recent great sexy experience. Just close your eyes for a moment and summon up what was the most sensual. Smell, of course, is one of the most powerful senses we possess. Should you catch a whiff of his cologne (even on somebody else!) your body will instantly associate it with the sensations of him moving inside you. If that doesn't make you glow, well, it might make you blush!

His voice in your ear is another glow-maker. If he's in the habit of whispering in your ear while making love, your body will program itself to respond to the sound of his voice, even over the telephone (have you tried phone sex?). When you have a lover, your body becomes attuned to all the senses involved and engaged during lovemaking—and it reacts with a Pavlovian response. Pavlov, you may remember, made dogs drool just by showing them some object they associated with pleasure. It follows that just laying eyes on her lover can make a woman go all pink and gooey.

Basically any sensual thing about lovemaking that helped to make her come (touch: his rough fingers in her vagina; taste: his semen; smell: the sweat on their entwined bodies; sound: his voice in her ear; sight: his penis moving in and out of her body) is a glow-extender.

By the way, men just live in their penises. Men have a sexual thought about every eight to ten seconds. Men don't need glow extenders. In any case, only about 30 percent of them experience sex afterglow.

PILLOW
talk

**Sex is a flame
which uncontrolled
may scorch;
properly guided,
it will light the
torch of eternity.**

−Joseph Fetterman

The French coined the phrase "69" or *Soixant-Neuf* in 1888.

Soixante-Neuf, commonly called 69, is the oral sex act of simultaneous pleasuring. It's the ultimate, you do me, I'll do you sex act. It does require a little skill to do correctly and a certain level of concentration. How it works is that each person's head is between the other person's thighs and that their tongues and fingers (if they like to use their hands) are working on each other's pleasure centers at the same time. A man and a woman can do it to each other; two women can do it, two men. It's called "69" because a "6" is the same thing as a "9" when they're reversed or upside down and this is the position that the two people duplicate when they do this thing.

The 69 move is prized as a sophisticated, highly erotic oral act because it is so packed with sensation. You have the moisture and the taste and the genital aromas and the body heat and that slightly

ILLOW *talk*

Nothing

is either

all masculine

or

all feminine

except

having sex.

—Marlo Thomas

claustrophobic feeling of being trapped between the other person's thighs, which ratchet up the erotic quotient of the experience. Plus it just feels so good! One problem associated with 69 is that while one person is enveloped in that degree of pleasure, they may forget that they've got work to do on their end. It's pretty tricky to concentrate on giving good head when you're receiving it at the same moment yourself. In the throes of ecstasy, the mind does tend to wander. While the ultimate in 69 is supposed to be simultaneous orgasm, from a more practical standpoint, it might be best when going for the gold to just take turns.

15

In Sydney, Australia, girls as young as seven are taught the fine art of pole-dancing as exercise.

Of course, proponents of the pole-dancing classes position it as a healthy alternative to not exercising, but the Australian Family Association argues they are inappropriate. In any case, young girls in Australia are able to emulate Britney Spears and other celebs by learning to strut their stuff at such a young age.

Ever wondered how they do it (and what they do when they do it) in far-flung locales? Take a look at some of these geographic sexual behaviors and then decide if it's worth updating your passport.

Brazil

Things are free and easy in swingin' Brazil where the two words "guilt" and "sex" are never said as one! Brazilians call condoms "camisinha," which means "small shirt." Even though hookups can happen at the drop of a hat, unmarried women and even adult guys live with their families well into their early thirties, so if you have a chance to go home with someone, know in advance, it'll probably have to happen at your hotel.

Egypt

In Egypt, a bride's virginity is so highly prized that doctors charge up to 1,000 Egyptian pounds to reconstruct a young woman's hymen.

Greece

Greeks are a very hot and passionate people—they're feisty and fiery! Anticipate that Greek men and women you meet might expect to have sex all night long, fortified by their national intoxicant, a booze called *restina*. Greek women also tend to be pretty busty, so if big breasts turn you on, head on out there!

Hungary

Hungary is the sex capital of the modern world. In fact, there are so many hookers in Budapest that it's driven the price of sex down. Budapest is also the most popular location for the international production of adult films. More mass-market, consumer-oriented porn is shot in Budapest than in any other place in the world. U.S. companies based in California's San Fernando Valley, which used to be the porn capital, now travel to Hungary to shoot their pictures because there's so much natural talent and the cost of production is so low.

Israel

Israeli girls are rough and tough because they've all been in the army. Expect them to kick butt! If you happen to be there and you're hoping for a hookup, understand that Israeli men and women are very forward and they might just hit on you first. It's a little harder to get lucky if you're not Jewish . . . but not impossible!

Japan

In Tokyo there's a fetish that was first made popular in the Harajuku district. It's called "Injured Idol." The fetish requires its practitioners (all healthy females) to wrap bandages around their heads and other body parts to attract men who are turned on by injured women.

Netherlands

Prostitution is legal in all of Holland, the most populous place to find sex for sale being Amsterdam. That city's Red Light District is famous for its prostitutes (female *and* male), who pose in windows to attract customers from all walks of life. As legal sex workers, prostitutes are required by law to pay taxes, be registered as sex workers, and submit to regular medical exams.

PILLOW *talk*

In America, sex is an *obsession*; in other parts of the world, it is *fact*.

—Marlene Dietrich

Seventy-three percent of women polled said they never used a vibrator. (They don't know what they're missing!)

In a study published in the journal *Sexually Transmitted Diseases,* which is being touted as the first academic survey of sex toy use, only 27 percent of participants report using sex toys. But the great thing about masturbation is that there's no wrong way to do it—whatever gets you off is the right way. Pocket rocket vibrators, clit ticklers, clever devices designed to be worn in your underwear, G-spot finders—they're all a lot of fun! Many women swear by the Hitachi Magic Wand, which features an impressive tennis ball–shaped head that can be inserted into the vagina. Doc Johnson's Ribbed Realistic Hard Throb is another insertion-oriented tool many ladies enjoy. The Impulse Jack Rabbit is so powerful that it has been rumored to render male partners obsolete! The Jack Rabbit has flickering clit-stimulating "rabbit ears," and a non-jamming beaded rotating

PILLOW talk

An

orgasm

a day

keeps the

doctor

away.

—Mae West

shaft with a seven-speed motor with six levels of rotation. If that sounds like too much of a good thing, or you don't like putting foreign objects inside your body, try Joanie's Butterfly or the Little Jelly Tickler instead. These two mini massaging vibrators are toys that many women love.

While using your hand is easy, cheap, and convenient, the advantage to using a vibrator is that you can sustain a level of intensity that the hand, which gets tired, just can't provide. Or you can use the vibrator to free up your hands to do other things, like caress your own breasts or tweak your nipples. Many women who aren't all that comfortable touching themselves often fall in love with their vibrators. And while some men object to their woman using a vibrator, take a tip from the wise man who said, "Real men aren't afraid of machinery."

Sometimes too much of a good thing can be a bad thing!

Yes. Excessive, persistent, intense sexual needs, urges involving nonhuman objects, and a need to masturbate constantly, are all considered psychological disorders! A fixation on masturbation is a compulsive sexual behavior, says the Mayo Clinic. Compulsive sexual behavior is known by other names such as hypersexuality, nymphomania, or erotomania. Some docs and shrinks call this behavior a sexual addiction, comparing it to the uncontrolled use of a drug. Some medical experts call excessive masturbation an issue of impulse control.

So how can you tell if you're playing with yourself too much? Here are the main questions: Does your your pleasuring routine interfere with your job? Would you rather stay home and masturbate than have a real social life or relate physically to your partner? Is staying home with your porn more important than hanging out with your friends? Do

PILLOW talk

You mustn't
force
sex
to do the work
of love or
love
to do the work
of sex.

—Mary McCarthy

you spend as much time as you can at work on the DL, furtively touching yourself while looking at smut on the web? If you've answered 'yes' to even one of these questions, you're masturbating too much!

Take a vacation from your self-pleasuring and spend more time in the company of other people. (But remember, there's no penalty attached to spending lots of time playing with yourself.)

44

Women have vibrators;
men have the "fleshlights."

Vibrating sex dolls, masturbation sleeves, and the "fleshlight" are all toys men can use to make their masturbation more interesting. A really wacky site called *www.homemade-sex-toys.com* has lots of inventive ideas for homemade sex toys that seem crazy but actually work! One idea involves scooping out a melon, heating it in a microwave, and lubing it up with KY. Another idea is to roll up a sock and then put a latex surgical glove inside it and then wrap the end of the glove over the top of the sock and lube it up. Put this thing between two pillows and hump away! Or you can drill a hole into a bar of soap, wet the soap and get busy. When the hole gets too big to stimulate your cock, just use it to wash off! But you're probably better off ordering a Pocket Pussy online, which is the bestselling sex toy for men that amazingly feels pretty much like the real thing—but doesn't ask you to sleep in the wet spot afterwards!

PILLOW
talk

We learn about
another's culture
the same way we
learn about sex:
in the streets.

–Ishmael Reed

In the Bible,
God killed Onan for pulling out.

In the Biblical book of Genesis, Onan, a Hebrew, was the second son of Judah. Interpretations of the narrative concerning Onan have resulted in the use of the term onanism, which means masturbation. The story of Onan goes that after God killed Onan's older brother, Er, Judah told Onan to have sex with Tamar, Er's widow, so that any resulting offspring could be declared as Er's heir. Still with me? Onan didn't object to having sex with Tamar, but he pulled out when he came, spilling his seed on the ground so that there couldn't be any offspring that he could not claim as his own. Obviously this act got him in a lot of trouble. The passage that describes this scene in the Old Testament says that the displeased Yahweh (God) then killed Onan for wantonly wasting his seed. The deaths of Onan and Er are among the very few deaths caused by

PILLOW talk

The major civilizing force in the world **is not** *religion,* **it is sex.**

—Hugh Hefner

Yahweh that the Torah doesn't describe as being caused by plague or the Angel of Death.

The early Christians just hated any wasting of seed because semen was considered divine and for the propagation of man. To have sex without the intention of procreation was considered a sin, an injury to nature. Roman Catholics cite the Onan narrative in the Bible as justification for bans against masturbation and coitus interruptus, that latter being the practice known as "pulling out." You may have noticed that while many Hebrew names from the Old Testament like Samuel and David and Daniel are popular names today, bet you can't think of one boy you ever met named Onan!

no.
20

When masturbating, lefties go to the left; righties go to the right.

According to the sex researchers Masters and Johnson, most women concentrate their efforts on one side of their clitoral shaft or the other. It's always the right if she's right-handed; the left if she's a southpaw. Women rarely manipulate the head of the clit, mostly because it's just too sensitive and tender. Some women pleasure themselves without even touching their clitoris at all because they find it too sensitive. Those women will touch themselves all around the tiny nub but never actually on it. Some women enjoy teasing their clitoris by only lightly touching it every third or fourth stroke and most women become very set in their ways about how they like their pleasuring.

This is why it takes a long time to break a new lover in, because you basically have to start from scratch to teach them how you like it. As for self-pleasuring, at the end of the day, every woman develops her own masturbation style—there's no right or wrong way to do it.

PILLOW *talk*

But did thee feel the earth move?

—Ernest Hemingway

no.
21

Five red-hot fantasies for women.

1. Believe it or not, having sex with a stranger is the most common female masturbation fantasy. At the same time, while this fantasy is very common, it takes a brave, bold woman to actually act it out! Such a person is always a big risk taker because, face it, sex with a total stranger is, by definition, risky!

   Back in the days of the French and English courts when masked balls were all the rage, a lady could dally with a stranger under the cover of disguise. Masked balls these days being in short supply, pulling off the reality of having sex with a stranger requires less ingenuity than guts. Mostly it means entering a bar and hooking up with the first cute guy you fancy. Grab him and take him out back for a quickie in the alley or in the loo in a locked stall. Sex with a stranger can be very exciting—

PILLOW *talk*

Nothing *risqué,* nothing gained.

–Alexander Woollcott

or very strange. You haven't a clue what the other person is into, which is part of the thrill of it!

2. Being dominated is another very common female fantasy. Most people imagine it's only submissive women who crave to be dominated, but that's dead wrong. Many bossy, somewhat bullying, pushy women have a not-so-secret desire to be pushed around! In fact, the more successful the woman is in her career and social standing, the more likely it is that in her psycho-sexual life, what she really wants is someone to dominate her. Psychologically speaking, she may require it to get off! If this sounds like you, you slightly over the top bully-girl, take charge by presenting your lover with a pair of velvet handcuffs, a ball gag, and a silk scarf. Inform your lover over cocktails about your wish to be dominated and how you crave calling him "master," but only in bed, of course. Unless he's totally dense or daft, he'll get the message! True, it is somewhat demanding and pushy to ask for what you want, (even if what you want is to be dominated), but if you don't take the initiative, your partner will never guess at your most secret and intimate desire!

3. Sex with your own partner doesn't sound like much of a fantasy, does it? Boring, boring, boring . . . not! People who have been together for a long time know exactly what it takes to tease and

please and totally pleasure their partner. No one knows you (and all your erogenous zones) better than the person who makes love with you all the time. Having sex with your own partner is an easy fantasy to make real. He's right there, lying beside you.

4. The "Mrs. Robinson" fantasy, that is, having sex with an inexperienced young man, better yet if he's a virgin, is the fantasy of many a naughty rule breaker. Is this boy "of age"? Be careful how you handle this fantasy if you choose to make it real. Women have been locked up for it!

5. Another red-hot female fantasy is to have sex with another woman. And no, having the fantasy (or even once in a while acting on it) doesn't make you a lesbian. Girl-on-girl action has a lot going for it. There's no fumbling around. No looking for that little man in the boat. No male ego to stroke! And since most men are eager to see their woman with another woman, this is a fantasy you can share with your partner. Think twice before rushing into making this fantasy a reality, because there will be consequences! For example, do not leap to make out with your best friend because if she is your best friend and the sex is incredible, you could wind up falling in love with each other! You do know what lesbians bring to a second date? A moving truck.

Masturbating at the start of a cycle can alleviate cramps.

According to Masters and Johnson in their classic clinical study, "Human Sexual Response," it was learned that women who masturbate themselves to orgasm shortly after the start of their menstrual cycle experience far less cramping and backache associated with menstruation than women who do not. The theory is that the increased flow of blood to the area and the pulsating, rolling wave effect of the orgasm is what gets rid of the cramps. So why wouldn't you just have sex with your partner? Because, um, vampire sex is so messy.

PILLOW
talk

I don't think

when I make love.

–Brigitte Bardot

23

Eight sexy things about chocolate.

Everybody knows that chocolate is delicious and tempting and semi-addictive and good to melt in your mouth. But did you know these important facts about chocolate and how it affects your sex life?

1. Chocolate is the food most commonly craved by women. Many women say they are as satisfied by a bar of chocolate or a bowl of chocolate ice cream as they are by sex! Chocolate may be the No. 1 sexual substitute for women who aren't gettin' any! No boyfriend in sight? Indulge!!

2. The Hershey Company introduced Milk Chocolate Hershey's Kisses in 1907. They are one of the most successful chocolates ever

produced. The Hershey Company makes approximately 25 million per day. That's a lot of Kisses!

3. Chocolate sauce poured on erogenous zones is fun (and tasty) to lick off. Avoid hairy areas, however, as chocolate-covered pubes are not cool to have stuck in your teeth!

4. The ancient Aztec Indians regarded chocolate as an aphrodisiac. For the Aztecs, chocolate truly was the food of love! Many South American and some European cultures have for hundreds of years used cocoa to treat diarrhea. That's not too sexy—but it works!

5. Chocolate's aphrodisiacal qualities can be attributed to two chemicals it contains. One is tryptophan, which is a building block of serotonin, a brain chemical involved in sexual arousal. The other is phenylethylamine, which is a stimulant related to amphetamine, which is released in the brain when people fall in love.

6. Chocolate stimulates the hypothalamus, which in turn produces sensations of pleasure in the brain and affects levels of serotonin. In high concentrations, however, serotonin can be converted to melatonin, which in large amounts reduces the sex drive. So while a little chocolate will turn you on, too much will turn you off!

7. Chocolate contains unsaturated N-acylethanolamines, which can activate cannabinoid receptors that result in heightened sensitivity and feelings of euphoria that feel to the body like love.

8. Chocolate is a sexy gift because it's such a familiar courtship ritual.

PILLOW *talk*

*A woman's appetite is **twice** that of a man's; her sexual desire, **four** times; her intelligence, **eight** times.*

—Sanskrit Proverb

no.
24

Five red-hot fantasies for men.

1. Most guys dream about being in a threesome; that would be two women and him. Who is servicing whom is what fuels the fantasy because in it the guy has two ladies, not one, attending to his needs. It's all about service! Two women fighting over him—what could be better? In this popular male fantasy, often depicted in adult films, the women should be getting it on a little with each other, not because they're really lesbians, but because they're putting on a show for their private audience, the guy.

2. Another popular male fantasy involves getting it on with a nurse or a strict schoolteacher. These fantasies are a bit about being dominated, because nurses and teachers are mild authority figures and

therefore "in charge." In the fantasy, the female must be a bossy bitch telling the man what he must do, things that might either hurt him a little or thrill him! If he's lucky, both! A nurse might also put on a rubber glove to explore the man's orifices . . . while he's on all fours, of course!

3. Making it with a schoolgirl is another major fantasy for a lot of guys. This fantasy is less a projection about real youth (after all, the guy isn't a pedophile) than it is about props and seductiveness masquerading as innocence. In this fantasy, clothes become really important. The woman should wear a classic schoolgirl outfit, like a little plaid skirt and knee highs. She should wear a headband or pull her hair into double ponytails.

4. Many men enjoy the idea of voyeurism, that is visualizing two other people getting it on with each other, or actually spying on a couple making love. Who doesn't like to watch? Voyeurism is an important part of our culture now, which is one of the reasons why we watch so many reality shows like *The Real World*, where cameras catch so much intimate stuff. The flip side of watching is showing off, and the "caught in the act" fantasy is a powerful one and a hot topic for exhibitionists. The act itself or who it's done with matters less than the thrill of

PILLOW talk

*Sex is **one** of the **nine** reasons for reincarnation. The other **eight** are unimportant.*

–Henry Miller

exposure. It's also a wild fantasy because public sex is against the law.

5. A lot of men love the idea of being videotaped during sex and fantasize about it because on some level, every guy thinks that, given the opportunity, he could become the next big sex star!

Nipples, genitals—and nostrils— swell during arousal.

That's because the inner nose, fine-tuned as it is to sensation and slight changes and gradations in pulse and body temperature, actually swells (very slightly) during sexual arousal. Check it out for yourself! Study your lover's face the next time you're making love and watch his or her nose grow . . . not exactly like Pinnochio's! Flared nostrils, by the way, are a dead giveaway to tell if someone is sexually interested in you. Whatever words come out of their mouth could be a lie, but the nose will tell the truth every time!

PILLOW *talk*

I remember
when the
air was *clean* and
the sex was *dirty*.

–George Burns

Semen is a low-calorie snack.

The average number of calories found in a teaspoon of semen is seven. While not exactly as low-cal as zero-calorie soda or vitamin-enhanced water, swallowing a load of semen won't affect your diet. Most men ejaculate between one and two teaspoons of semen at a time. Ejaculate production varies daily from man to man. Some make more. Some less! For the record, it's been estimated that the average number of times a man will ejaculate in his lifetime is 7,200.

PILLOW *talk*

It is with our
passions, as it is
with fire and water,
they are good
servants but
bad masters.

—Aesop

Richard Branson, owner of Virgin Atlantic Airways, claims to have joined the Mile High Club in 1969 at the age of nineteen.

The Mile High Club (*www.milehighclub.com*) is a club, or at least the idea of a club, whose members claim to have had sex in an airplane with another person while being at an altitude of no less than 5,280 feet. That's a mile above the earth—hence the name!

Veteran pilots say that to be a member of the club, you have to be at the controls of the airplane at the time, but over the years, the "club" has expanded its criteria to include membership of people who make it in airplane lavatories aboard jetliners traversing the world. Despite the website, there is no official Mile High organization or club, and the rules listed on the website are for entertainment purposes only, or, in other words, completely bogus. And yet the club seems real, if only because so many people go on the site and post detailed messages about their in-flight, sky-high adventures. So you might say the club is a living, breathing urban legend.

Richard Branson, owner of Virgin Atlantic Airways, claims to have joined the Mile High Club in 1969 at the age of nineteen when he engaged in sex with a married woman in an airplane lavatory. In 2007 a Qantas flight attendant named Lisa Robertson claimed to have had sex with the actor Ralph Fiennes in a business-class lavatory. The BBC ran a report investigating whether or not sex on a plane was illegal. The report concluded that any legalities have more to do with whether or not anyone saw you having sex, since public sex and indecent exposure are illegal. To satisfy the public's desire to join the mythological Mile High Club, some commercial airlines have instituted special charter flights to fulfill the purpose, and by selling souvenir certificates and other items related to sex in the sky. It's fun to log on to the website and read about other people's adventures . . . or post your own if you've had some.

PILLOW
talk

When she raises her eyelids it's as if she were taking off all her clothes.

—Collette

It takes up to four hours of vigorous sex to burn off the calories in one slice of pizza.

While there's a widely held belief that a half hour of energetic sex burns the equivalent calories in a slice of pizza, it's just not true. Let's look at the math: a half hour of vigorous sex burns about 85 calories, and most diet websites say that a slice of plain cheese pizza is about 230 calories, while a slice of pepperoni is about 290 calories. So, it's pretty clear that it takes more than thirty minutes of active lovemaking to burn off a single slice. Even guys on Viagra can't have sex for hours on end, so don't count on *that* to help you lose weight—unless your motivation to lose weight is to look better while having sex. In which case, simply nix the pizza!

PILLOW *talk*

Sex is the great amateur art.

—David Cort

29

The Jade Flute adds "music" to lovemaking.

It's been documented that there are more than 600 positions, postures, and poses that can be assumed making love. It would take an entire lifetime of sex to try everything, not to mention the athletic ability of an Olympian gymnast and the stamina of a racehorse! Many complex sexual positions are a lot like yoga poses (by the way, yoga can be instrumental to great sex because it makes you so flexible!).

In many cultures (notably none of them American), a great deal of scholarship, practice, and energy has been devoted to the art of love. Beautiful, fanciful names were given at one time to sexual positions that are rarely practiced in our country or for the most part, anywhere in contemporary culture. Many of these positions may seem very strange, even freakish, although most are just minor variations on commonly practiced positions and sexual themes.

The Jade Flute is an ancient and revered Asian love-making technique, perfected by pricey prostitutes and geishas. Essentially it's an orally enhanced hand job. How to do it? The woman sits astride him (he's naked; she can be naked or clothed) and takes his penis in both hands, her fingers at the top of the shaft and her thumbs placed underneath. Sort of like how you'd hold a flute, come to think of it! While her fingers are arranged in this position, she pumps (slow at first and then as his excitement warrants, faster and faster) his penis with her hands, while her mouth caresses his shaft with her lips and tongue.

The technique was originally conceived to pump up and bolster an old guy's penis, but it works on any one that's slow-to-rise. The technique also makes it the ideal sex act between acts, meaning you've already had sex and now you're taking a breather, but this is what you do when you're wanting more and need to fire him up again. The hand also provides an assist to the mouth to prop up the penis in case it starts to flag, and also relieves the fatigue out of all the oral work! Try it!

PILLOW *talk*

Lord,

make me chaste—

but not yet.

–St. Augustine

About 30 percent of males in the world are circumcised.

Male circumcision is the surgical removal of some or all of the foreskin or prepuce of the penis. The word comes from the Latin word *caedere* which means "to cut." While the practice is very old (there are cave drawings depicting it), circumcision is a religious commandment for those who practice Judaism or who live by the rules of the Islamic culture. Circumcision is also a requirement of the Oriental Orthodox Christian church in Africa. According to the World Health Organization, about 30 percent of males in the world are circumcised. At the same time, human foreskin is a highly innervated, vascularized, sensitive erogenous zone. It would seem obvious that removal of the foreskin interferes with sexual function and pleasure, and yet studies abound for and against circumcision.

The Centers for Disease Control in 2008 cited evidence that male circumcision significantly reduces the risk of HIV, and at the same time clearly noted that the procedure provides only partial protection and should not replace other interventions known to prevent transmission of that disease. Research from the American Academy of Pediatrics, the Masters and Johnson Institute, and the American Academy of Family Physicians suggests there is little discernable difference in experiencing pleasure between circumcised and uncircumcised males.

Nevertheless, a preponderance of anecdotal evidence is published on and off the web decrying the practice of what many call "the unkindest cut of all." Citing that the genitally intact male has thousands of fine touch receptors and other highly erogenous nerve endings, it would seem that these pleasure-producers would be lost to circumcision. But since anti-circumcision studies are often biased, and much of the medical literature on the subject is contradictory, at the end of the day, sexual pleasure remains a personal and highly subjective emotional, physical, psychological, even spiritual, experience.

PILLOW
talk

As a matter
of biology, if
something bites
you it is probably
feminine.

—Scott M. Kruse

The original Kama Sutra was written in Sanskrit between the second and fourth centuries A.D.

The Kama Sutra, frequently referred to as the "bible" of sex, is an ancient tome, a relic. It is believed to have been written by an Indian gentleman called Mallanaga from the esteemed Vatsayayana family of India. Mallanaga lived sometime between the first and the fourth centuries A.D., and he wrote in Sanskrit, the ancient classical language of India and of Hinduism.

Although the Kama Sutra flourished as the book of love in India for centuries, it was virtually unknown in the Western world until Sir Richard Burton (not the actor) and F. F. Arbuthnot, two friends in Victorian England, founded the Kama Sutra Society. They did this as an excuse to study Hindu erotic literature. Arbuthnot was a retired civil servant and Burton was a published writer. The two men elected to reorganize Mallanaga Vatsayayana's 1,000 chapters into a more manageable 150. It is their version that is the most widely used, imitated, and plagiarized. Truly a scholarly textbook on making love, the Kama Sutra discusses positions, how and where to kiss, love bites, more positions, and likens the mating of humans to different species of birds and beasts. For example, do you fornicate more like a mare who has foaled many times, a rutting boar, or are you more quick and sparrow-like? The original translation by Burton and Arbuthnot also goes into great detail about boudoir courtesies and the social etiquette regarding copulation with courtesans, eunuchs, and women who aren't your wife.

PILLOW *talk*

Sex is like money; only **too much** *is* **enough.**

—John Updike

The prize for sexiest animal goes to the female pig.

You've heard the expression, "fuck like bunnies," and it's known that cats even have sex with their mothers and their brothers! But female pigs can have orgasms that last up to thirty minutes! Lucky pig! (On the other hand, it's physically impossible for a pig to look up at the sky and count stars. So go figure.)

PILLOW
talk

His finest hour lasted a minute and a half.

—Phyllis Diller

33

The longest penis recorded by anthropologists measures 17 inches long.

The late, great porn star John Holmes, aka Johnny Wadd, star of more than 2,800 adult films, was said to have possessed a penis measuring 10 to 12 inches when erect. The longest penis recorded by anthropologists studying tribes found that the Caramojas of Northern Uganda and the Mambas of New Hebrides have men whose penises measure 17 inches long. Caramoja males are practitioners of that weird thing where the men wrap their penises in yards of cloth and ritually stretch them. These guys really do walk around with their cocks hanging to their knees! Is it attractive? You'd probably have to be a Caramoja woman to answer that!

As a rule, men tend to exaggerate the size of their penises. When a man tells you the length of his penis, ask him if he's measuring from the shaft (or root), or from the glans to the gonads. Penis length differs wildly depending on where you hold the tape.

ILLOW *talk*

The natural man has only two primal passions— to get and beget.

–William Osier

Essential oils can be potent aphrodisiacs.

Aphrodisiacs are aromatic foods, recipes, and potions believed to be sexual and sensual enhancers found in nature. Many of these potent love tools and libido lifters have been in use for centuries. The ancient Greeks and Romans were a hedonistic bunch, as were the Taoist Chinese and the Tantric Hindus. There are dozens of known aphrodisiacs in the world, many of them essential oils that can be easily found. Ylang ylang is an essential oil that is derived from the flower that has the same name. The word itself means "flower of flowers." Used as aromatherapy, ylang ylang is thought to be a sexual healer. The finest oils come from the yellow flowers, although the plants also bloom in shades of mauve and pink. How it works: Physiologically, ylang ylang slows down the pulse and steadies a heart that's beating irregularly due to stress. The oil is also thought to be a soother to the emotions, as it is a natural antidepressant and relaxant.

Sandalwood, another essential oil, is an aromatherapeutic tool. Prized as the "perfume of love," sandalwood is popularly used in massage on the breasts as an energizer and around the genitals to soothe inflammation. In India, the Hindu god Indra is always depicted with his breast painted with sandalwood oil. On the subject of breasts and essential oils, in the Far East, women with small breasts are advised to rub them with a mixture of geranium, ylang ylang, camellia, and clary sage. This is supposed to be a plumping agent that also tones flabby breasts.

Nineteenth-century prostitutes used a mixture of vanilla, rose, and jasmine to make a perfume recipe called "Follow Me Boy," which was believed to improve business. Street walkers rubbed it on their bodies to attract men. It's easy enough to mix up a batch yourself and test it out on your regular partner. A word of warning: it smells very sweet!

Jojoba oil rubbed directly on the vagina is a natural lubricant.

Lavender, bergamot, ravansara, and tea tree oils mixed with 100 milligrams of spring water makes an excellent douche. It's best used to clear up any irritation caused by an abundance of vigorous lovemaking.

 **PILLOW** *talk*

What do I wear in bed? Why, Chanel No. 5 of course.

—Marilyn Monroe

no.
35

Oysters can get you hot—
but so can celery!

Many aphrodisiacs can be found at the grocery store. Walnuts are thought to be beneficial in terms of fertility. The ancient Romans believed that tossing them at a newly married couple was a guarantee they'd soon be conceiving. Walnuts are a powerful source of vitamins and minerals that build up and support the immune system—good for sex!

Celery has a long history of being a food of love. It contains the vitamins A, B, C, and D and loads of minerals. The seeds themselves are thought to be an actual aphrodisiac. Also celery is mostly water and is hydrating. Plus if you eat it instead of crackers or chips, you'll stay sexy slim!

Fresh figs were enjoyed by the ancient Greeks as a prelude to sex orgies. Not only are they dripping with nectar, but the shape looks a lot like the inside of the female vulva, which is also pulpy and pink.

Caviar is a famous aphrodisiac. Real caviar comes from the eggs of the sturgeon, an ancient bony fish native to subtropical, temperate, and subarctic rivers, lakes, and coastlines of Eurasia and North America. Caviar is a luxury food, and rare, too, as many of the fish that create the best roe are on the endangered species list due to over-harvesting and high luxury consumer demand. Caviar contains large amounts of the vitamins A, D, B_1, B_2, and B_6, and phosphorous, all of which are known stimulants to the circulatory system. Circulation being integral to orgasm, this makes caviar a proven aphrodisiac. A bit of advice if you're allergic to fish eggs or are a vegetarian: you can get all these vitamins and phosphorous at the health food store. Love caviar? Try eating it on toast points with chopped hard-boiled egg and a tiny bit of onion. Heavenly when served with icy cold champagne!

Oysters are not called the food of love for nothing. Pure protein, they are an energy booster that, unlike pasta, won't leave you feeling stuffed. Eat 'em raw on the half shell, bathed in their own salty juice, a brine that closely resembles a woman's vaginal juices when she's hot and aroused. Oysters are always linked with the idea of horniness and indeed ordering them to share between a couple is practically a prelude to a sex act. You slurp them down whole, and they're an acquired taste, like learning to love giving head or some other practice-makes-perfect experience. Last but not least, oysters are loaded with zinc. Male porn stars take zinc every day to keep up their professional studliness, or they take Viagra. You don't need a prescription for zinc, however.

Chocolate was actually banned from monasteries centuries ago because it was considered too sexy! Chocolate contains caffeine, which is a stimulant, and theobromine, also known to raise the blood pressure. Chocolate also contains phenylethylamine, a natural amphetamine. The combination of all these natural drugs makes chocolate a food that gives you a lift. Neuroscientists say that chocolate contains pharmacologically active substances that have a similar effect on the brain as marijuana. While it doesn't exactly get you high, chocolate does give a person that warm and fuzzy feeling also associated with love and sex. At the same time chocolate is

PILLOW *talk*

I wasn't **kissing** *her.*
I was **whispering** *in her mouth.*

—Chico Marx

relaxing, and eating a great deal of it has been shown to lower inhibitions. Watch out!

Ginger is an aphrodisiac because it gives the eater a slight flush. All over the world, ginger has been used to spike a lady's drink to naturally stimulate her. Makes you feel a bit differently now about ginger ale now, doesn't it?

Two more food tips: Eating a lot of watermelon will make semen and vaginal secretions taste sweeter. Eating asparagus will do the opposite. Don't like that rank smell your pee gets after eating a few spears? Then definitely don't eat asparagus if you think you'll be making love after dinner!

Sometimes it's okay to play with "scissors" in bed!

Another French position known as the *flanquette* asks that partners arrange themselves so that the woman lies facing the man with one of her legs between his, and one of his legs between hers. Think scissors. It's a high school wrestling move. The benefit to this position is that extra clitoral pressure is achieved by the man's thigh when he presses down with it. That also puts pressure on the area of her G spot, which will spontaneously result in a more profound female orgasm. So this is a female-friendly position, conceived to increase *her* pleasure. (Think of it as a she-comes-first thing.)

PILLOW
talk

**While a person does
not give up on sex,
sex does not give up
on the person.**

—Gabriel Garcia Marquez

Squeezing a partner to orgasm solely with the vaginal muscles is what the French call *pompoir.*

Pompoir is a fancy French name for "Kegel," as in Kegel exercises recommended by most OB-GYNs to patients who have just given birth. The exercises, which involve internal squeezing of the vagina, strengthen the pelvic muscles and the entire pelvic floor. A woman who is able to squeeze a man to orgasm this way is considered to be a very accomplished, sophisticated, and prized love partner! Strengthening the internal muscles by Kegeling has also been proven to cure incontinence. There's a multitude of benefits to be reaped by mastering this technique, so absolutely practice hard and practice often!

PILLOW
talk

I think that making love is the best form of exercise.

—Cary Grant, American actor

The "lazy" position
is not what it seems. . . .

It's not about having sex while you're watching the tube or simultaneously munching a bag of Doritos or talking on the phone. Although that is lazy! And rude! Or both!

The lazy position is one recommended by sex therapists as a cure for partial impotence. It's a favorite among older men or guys on medication (high blood pressure, high cholesterol, anti-anxiety meds, for instance) that have a bit of difficulty raising and keeping it up. How you work it is that both partners recline, spoon-style, on their sides. The woman draws one leg up and sticks her bottom out. The man enters from behind. This position can be managed even when the man has a very limited erection, or in some cases, barely any erection at all. It's also a good choice for heavyset or slightly disabled folks. The most important part of the position is that it's a booster for male morale.

PILLOW *talk*

Women might
be able to fake
orgasms. But men
can fake *whole*
relationships.

–Sharon Stone

39

Many men really get off when a woman talks dirty in bed.

They find it arousing! And there are plenty of women out there who wish their guy would talk dirty to them, too. The trouble is, most people who are well-mannered and well-trained are seriously uncomfortable with this kind of communication, plus they don't really know what to say! Study this primer on how to be a better potty mouth and see if you don't reap the benefits the next time you're in bed!

Problem: I'd like my boyfriend to whisper filthy things in my ear when we're in bed, but he doesn't know what to say. In fact, he says he finds that kind of talk to be just hilarious! What should I do to remedy this situation?

Problem Solved: Instead of laughing at your boyfriend's helplessness, what you need to do is get serious. First stretch your naked or nearly naked self up alongside him and whisper in your throatiest voice in his ear exactly and explicitly what you would like him to say to you. For example, tell him what spot on your body would most appreciate a tonguing. Then explain that you require a running dialogue from him describing how you look, smell, and taste. That should get the message across!

Problem: What's a good way to ask for dirty talk—bearing in mind I'm really embarrassed about my need to hear it?

Problem solved: Take an academic approach and set up a schedule. On Day 1 you will say something flirtatiously filthy to your lover. Possibly you will tell him how much you like his penis and how large it is. On Day 2 you will describe a fantasy you have about your boyfriend and then ask him to tell you a fantasy of his own. On Day 3 you will practice saying every slang word you know for female genitalia out loud and ask him to repeat back the words. On Day 4 you will read together a passage from an erotic novel. By Day 5 your inhibitions about giving and getting dirty talk should be history. As they say, practice makes perfect.

Problem: My man is happy to talk dirty—but he's so bad at it it doesn't turn me on at all—how do I tell him what I want without hurting his feelings?

Problem solved: When you've got him in a nice lubricated mood and the lights are turned down low and you're both feeling randy, nicely tell your boyfriend that certain words or phrases he uses which he means to be sexy are instead turning you off! Before he goes into major pout mode and threatens to never say one more sexy thing to you again, offer him suggestions of what you would like him to say. Give clear-cut examples. Give him the exact words and phrases that turn you on. If you tell him this while you are doing something sexy, like stroking his inner thigh, he'll be much more receptive about hearing your message. Carry on from there!

Problem: I want to talk dirty but I don't want to sound like a bad erotic thriller—how do I get it right?

Problem solved: Lacking the confidence to say the right things on your own, feel free to borrow dialogue from somebody else! Watching erotic movies or programs on cable TV and stealing dialogue directly from those sources is perfectly legit. Have no qualms about taking hot dialogue straight out of erotic books. Your partner will never know that your most erotic utterings aren't your own! The funny thing about learning to talk dirty is that gradually, with practice, you will be able to generate your own raunchy talk. Speak from the heart, or, er, the clitoris, and you can't fail to be inspired.

ILLOW *talk*

Sex in a car.

If I were in a really raunchy frame of mind wanting something crazy and kinky, the back seat would be it.

—Scarlett Johansson

no.

40

"Dining at the Y" is a euphemism for cunnilingus.

Dining at the Y or the YMCA is a cheeky way to describe any oral sex where the vagina is being pleasured. The 'Y' refers to the anatomical geography between a woman's legs where they join at the southern region of her torso. Viewed from above, the pubic area resembles an inverted Y. The slang phrase "Dining at the Y" became popular after it was used on the Showtime drama, *The L Word,* where the cast of lesbian characters often discuss eating tuna tacos, bearded clams, loose meat sandwiches, and snapper. Other vernacular to describe the act of going down on a woman are muff diving, muffin- and muff-barking.

Analingus, which is not exactly Dining at the Y, but more like slipping around the corner for dessert or a side dish, is also called rimming. Rimming is oral sex where one person licks the other person's anus. The combination of cunnilingus and anal-oral copulation is often

called "tossing the salad," which is sexual contact between one person's mouth and anus and perineum and the vagina of the other. Oral-anal sex is also sometimes called "tonguing the tan track." Engaging in these oral acts are pleasurable to many—both heteros and homos can enjoy it.

*There may be some things **better** than sex, and there may be some things **worse**. But there's nothing quite like it.*

—W C Fields

no.
41

Female hyenas have balls and mating squid do it 24/7 for two weeks!

Female hyenas are the bosses of the pack. They are much bigger and stronger than the males and definitely more aggressive. Plus they've got balls—for real! Female hyenas also have a pseudopenis, that is an enlarged clitoris that they can erect on command. The far smaller and meeker male has to insert his penis into her pseudopenis—that is, if she'll let him. This is a tricky business for the guys, but nothing compared to the trial the gals have to go through when they have to give birth through their false dicks.

Male dolphins have a retractable penis that also swivels. This swiveling penis is also what they call "prehensile," meaning they can use their cock like a hand. Male dolphins have an extremely strong sex drive and can mate many times in a day. Here's the downside. For all their action, male dolphins are not exactly studs. The average time frame for dolphin intercourse is twelve seconds before the males shoot their wad.

Male dolphins are also kind of stupid since they will try to hump inanimate objects and other species of animals. Sea turtles: watch your back! They're also gang bangers; when a pack of dolphin males happen upon a female, they will surround her and try to force her to have sex.

Girl and boy hippos attract their mates by marking their territory by urinating and defecating at the same time. A love-struck hippo will swirl its tail around like a lasso to spread this awful stuff. When a likely pair do meet, drawn by their stinky aromas, their foreplay involves finding a pond or other body of water where they can spend a couple of hours together splashing around. Only after they've bathed together, do the two hippos make love.

A pair of mating squid do it all day long—for two weeks. Mating squid only take a break from their lovemaking enough for the females to dive down to deposit their fertilized eggs. And they only have sex during daylight, using the evenings and nights to eat and rest up.

Male porcupines douse their love object with their urine to let her know she's the one. Then it's up to the female to accept or object to the courtship. If she's not ready to get it on with him, the female will verbally abuse the male, striking him, even biting him to express her displeasure. This courtship can last for up to six months! When the female is finally ready to accept the guy's entreaties, the quills of both parties relax and go flat. Then the male enters her from behind and they screw until the male is exhausted. If the female wants to continue, she will mate with any male who gave her a squirt who she likes. To cool down, the female acts out the entire courtship process but in reverse, which means she's the one squirting urine at the guy.

Geese are into threesomes. Many male geese develop homosexual relationships, preferring their own company to that of a female. But should a gal goose be in the mood to make some goslings, she will court the two males until one of them fertilizes her eggs. Then the three stay together as long as it takes to attend to the tiny newborns, whom they all raise.

It's been estimated that between 8 and 14 percent of seagulls are lesbians. The couple go through all the mating behaviors of hetero seagulls, except they lay sterile eggs. Other species with large numbers of homosexuals in their ranks include squid, rats, monkeys, geese, and ostriches.

PILLOW *talk*

I need **more sex,** *OK? Before I die I wanna taste* **everyone** *in the world.*

—Angelina Jolie

42

Sex can land you in the slammer.

Sex by its very nature is risky! One minute you're having a good time, and then next minute, out come the handcuffs! Lots of sex acts are illegal and in many parts of the world the rules change from border to border. To steer clear of the law, bone up on some of these rules and regulations regarding the buying of sex, the selling of sex, sex acts that are considered in some places too lewd or profane. Why is it so important to know all this stuff? Because when you're standing in front of a judge over some matter that involves fornication, there is one basic rule of thumb: "Ignorance is no excuse."

You can only sell condoms from vending machines in the state of Maryland as long as alcoholic beverages are also sold on the same premises.

Crimes Against Nature, a North Carolina General Statute, Section 14-177, are still on the books. Crimes Against Nature are sex acts deemed to be "contrary to the order of nature," and cover anything considered "bestial," such as oral sex and anal intercourse. Luckily, these laws, while obviously broken all the time, hardly ever result in having to make an appearance in court.

Also in North Carolina, any two people having sex who are not married to each other are fornicating, which is against the law. It's a Class 2 misdemeanor, by the way.

It's illegal anywhere in the United States to have sex with a corpse.

You can be arrested in Indiana for walking around in public with a hard-on even if your clothes are covering you up. Being in a "turgid state" is not acceptable in Indiana!

In Oklahoma if you promise to marry a virgin and then have sex and don't marry her, you're in a heap of trouble! You could go to jail for five years! But if you're arrested and then apologize and go back and marry her, all is forgiven at once.

Adultery in Idaho can get you thrown in jail for three years and might cost you $1,000.

Any sexual position except for the missionary position is technically illegal in Maryland.

Prostitution is legal but regulated in Switzerland, New Zealand, the Netherlands, and Nevada. Registered prostitutes in Nevada must undergo monthly checks for HIV and condoms are mandatory for all oral sex

PILLOW *talk*

Sex:

The thing that takes up the least amount of time and causes the most amount of trouble.

—John Barrymore

and intercourse. Brothel owners are liable if any customer becomes infected with HIV from a woman working at that brothel.

The age of consent in Alabama is sixteen. The age of consent in Mexico is twelve.

Any man or woman caught fornicating with a male animal in Lebanon is going straight to jail. It is not illegal, however, to have sex with a female animal.

In Islamic countires, you better never ever look at a dead person's private parts. No Muslim, not even if he's a doctor or an undertaker, can look at a dead person's entire naked body. A Muslim male doctor can't look at the uncovered breasts or genitals of any woman, save for his wife.

43

There's a link between boating and the clitoris.

The clitoris is sometimes called "the man in the boat," because that's what it looks like, a little individual in a canoe, the labia being the canoe, the clit the man. The clitoris is made up of erectile tissue wrapped around the vagina and the urethra, which swells with blood when aroused. The clitoris is actually much larger than it looks when viewed with a mirror or through the eyes of someone positioned between your legs. Unless you're using MRI equipment and can actually see inside the body, all that can be seen of the clitoris is the tip or the glans.

The "man" part of the "man in the boat" description is actually quite apt as the clitoris has a lot in common with the penis. Some women have very large and pronounced clitorises, especially female body builders who take steroids. (Taking steroids will give you a giant clit.) Having a big clit may or may not make you hotter or hornier or enhance your

PILLOW talk

In gardens, beauty is a by-product. The main business is **sex** *and* **death**.

—Sam Llewelyn

sexual pleasure (although it does stand to reason that the more of something there is, the merrier), but it will enable a top woman to grind her clit into her female partner's crotch so that they can have sex that's more like the traditional male/female equation.

Speaking of men, most guys are thrilled to find a woman with an extra large clit and find an oversized organ very sexy. That could be because the guy is just happy to encounter a vagina with a clitoris he doesn't have to hunt around for.

The word "orgy," comes from the Greek word *orgia*, meaning "secret rites" (and other sexual ephemera).

The term "orgy" originally denoted the secret rites and ceremonies connected to the worship of deities like Bacchus and Dionysus. The first orgies were restricted only to the fairer sex. Evidently, back in the glory days of Greece and Rome, it was often the girls' night out to shout.

The classic French term for a three-way is *ménage a trois.*

Lots of ladies have an extra nipple, but only 1 out of 4,000 has an extra breast. Polymazia, or polymastia, is a medical condition where a third breast appears on the body. It doesn't have to be between the other breasts. It could come out in an odd location, like the armpit. The condition is actually more common in men! Polymazia is considered by doctors to be a congenital abnormality, but abnormal can be beautiful in the eye of the right beholder. Anne Boleyn, the second wife of Henry VIII, is said to have had it, and until she lost her head was considered to be a great beauty. Of course when Henry had her charged with witchcraft and conjuring, that third teat probably became a liability.

Tiny studs surgically embedded in the shaft of the penis for the purpose of enhancing sexual pleasure is the custom of some people in India, who call this, "the wooden mortar." The idea is that the bumps create a different kind of friction in the vagina and this increases pleasure. Why you wouldn't just wear a bump-enhanced condom is unclear. Seems unlikely that this far-out, Far East sexual practice will catch on in the United States.

Upper-crust gentlemen of the Victorian era had their penises pierced with a "dressing ring," to firmly secure their genitalia to either the right or the left, depending on which side they "dressed." The reason? To prevent unsightly bulges.

Speaking of penis piercing, the most classic pierce through the urethra and the glans is called a Prince Albert.

PILLOW *talk*

When a man goes on a date, he *wonders* if he is going to get lucky. A woman *already knows*.

—Frederike Ryder

The F-word is universally understood in just about any language.

While there are definitely specific slang words or phrases that mean sexual congress, such as *foutre* or *niquer* in French, and *jodete* in Spanish, meaning "fuck you," or *hacete coger*, which is Spanish for "go get fucked," and *das war ein geiler fick*, which means "that was a great fuck" in German, or the equally wonderful *verpiss dich*, which is German for "fuck off," the plain unadorned word "fuck" seems to be understood in every dialect, including Chinese, Japanese, and Urdu. Why is that? Probably because the word is so simple to say and has such a satisfying ring to it.

PILLOW
talk

One half of
the world cannot
understand the
understand the
pleasures of
the other.

–Jane Austen

The alleged rape committed by Roman Polanski took place at the Bel Air mansion of his good friend, Jack Nicholson.

Roman Polanski, filmmaker and former husband of Sharon Tate (who was murdered in their Benedict Canyon home by members of the Charles Manson gang), the guy who directed *Rosemary's Baby* and *Chinatown*, was in 1977 arrested for the rape of a thirteen-year-old girl.

The story goes that Polanski had arranged to take photos of the girl, Samantha Geimer, in her swimsuit for French *Vogue*. The shoot (and alleged rape) took place at the Bel Air mansion of Polanski's good friend Jack Nicholson. Following a dip in the hot tub, prosecutors said Polanski gave the girl quaaludes and champagne and the two had sex. The girl told her mother about her afternoon and the mom called the police. Polanski was ordered by the court to undergo examination as a mentally disordered offender.

Accepting a plea bargain, he agreed to one count of unlawful sex with a minor even though there were six counts against him at his arraignment. Facing three years in prison, Polanski hopped a plane and fled to France before the sentencing, and has not set foot in the United States since. In 2003 he won the Academy Award for his direction of *The Pianist*.

PILLOW *talk*

A

dirty book

is

rarely

dusty.

—Unknown

The Spanish have more than 100 words for the male member.

There are a fair share of English words, too! Cock, dick, Johnson, willy, phallus, pizzle (that's Australian), the male member, sausage, tool, weiner, woody, shlong, stiffy, skin flute, snake, prick, pud, shaft, pecker, package, dong, dork, joystick, and peter are the most common slang terms in the English language to describe a penis. Phallus is actually a medical term, not a slang one. Common terms in other languages to describe the male member are "blo" (Armenian), "bun jou" (Cantonese), "piktrompet"(Danish), "burat" (Filipino), "bod" (Gaelic/Irish), "lingum" (Hindi/Urdu), "frusta la carne"(Italian), and "kuk" (Norwegian). The French have about 100 slang terms for penis; Germans about half that. The Spanish have different words in differ-ent dialects including Colombian, Chilean, Argentinian, and Panamanian. Among the most colorful terms are "machete" (that's Venezuelan), matacuaza (Mexican), and "pedro," (that's "peter" in Spanish). There are literally hundreds if not a thousand words for the male member!

PILLOW talk

*I think I could fall **madly** in bed with you.*

—Unknown

One stamp-sized piece of foreskin contains enough genetic material to grow 200,000 units of faux skin.

Ever wonder what happens to all those babies' foreskins after they've been removed? Hospitals sell them to pharmaceutical companies and laboratories for bio-research who use them for clinical investigation and the growing field of artificial skin technology.

PILLOW
talk

Tell him I've been too fucking busy—

or vice versa.

–Dorothy Parker

D. H. Lawrence's *Lady Chatterley's Lover* supplies ideas for how to master erotic talk.

Face it. It can be tricky to talk to a new lady about her vagina. Take your lead from how she talks about it herself. This is a classic case of monkey see, monkey do, or more accurately given the situation, monkey hear, monkey repeat. A lot of women are really touchy about what they call their vagina, and can also be sensitive about what their partner calls it. To find out what she calls it, listen carefully. In the heat of the moment, did she cry out, "My pussy's so hot for you?" If so, call her pussy a pussy.

A surprising number of women don't have any name for their lady parts at all. They call it "it," as in giving the direction, "Lick it," when they want you to eat them out. If you can't catch a clue, ask her what she calls it, offering in exchange info on what you call your cock. This is what's called a "Lady Chatterley's Lover" conversation since in D. H. Lawrence's novel, giving names to her vagina and his penis was the illicit lovers' pastime.

PILLOW *talk*

The tragedy is when
you've got sex in
the head instead of
down there where
it belongs.

—D. H. Lawrence

Ancient Romans regarded threesomes as the ultimate demonstration of sexual pleasure.

The threesome—that is three individuals having sex with each other all at the same time—spans the ages. The Greeks, the Romans, and the Etruscans all enjoyed themselves with threesomes, absolute proof that three's *not* a crowd. In fact, sex with more than one person at a time can be sublime.

The classic threesome in modern western culture has evolved over the years. Although humans have always been interested in threesomes, the practice first came to national attention in the psychedelic 1960s when alternative lifestyle publications and soft-core porn magazines such as *Playboy*, *Penthouse*, and *Hustler* turned their focus to group sex. The classic combination for decades was a man with two women, with the penis as the connecting point and the women playfully fighting over it. Commonly in this combination, the women engage in a bit of lightweight sex with each other, mostly to further stimulate the man. In recent years, however, the most popular combination for a threesome is a woman with two men. That is because the focus has shifted to female pleasure, with the goal of seeing how many orgasms she can have. In this combination, the men customarily do not engage in sexual activity with each other and must orchestrate and choreograph their bodies to avoid physical contact. Although the men are expected to come, their role is primarily to satisfy the woman and to stimulate and penetrate her multiple orifices at one time. Of course, gay and lesbian threesomes are quite a different matter, as everyone is ideally both on the giving and the receiving end of pleasure at all times.

How one might go about organizing a threesome can be tricky. Generally speaking, in committed heterosexual relationships, the woman is far less likely to agree to a threesome unless she gets to call all the shots. Any husband or boyfriend who dreams of participating in a threesome should first introduce the notion into his wife or girlfriend's mind, and then, if she doesn't become furious and threaten to kill him, permit her to decide when and where and with whom the thing could happen. A word to the wise man: never anticipate getting permission to make love to your wife's best friend. The two women may adore each other and share all their secrets, but it's highly unlikely your wife will be willing to share *you*.

PILLOW
talk

An erection is like

the Theory

of Relativity—

the more you

think about it,

the harder it gets.

–Unknown

Many swinging couples are into threesomes and are looking for a single man (or woman) to get it on with.

A national site called *www.swingersclublist.com* provides an excellent resource for how to, er, get in the swing, and find out what the swinging lifestyle is all about. Traveling? You can select a world region by clicking on a map, so if you happen to be on business in South America, chances are good that you can find a hookup. Swingers, you will quickly surmise, can be found everywhere and they're not always couples. Many swinging couples are into threesomes and are looking for a single man (or woman) to get it on with.

In the U.S., the swinging lifestyle, as it is more commonly known (and just for the record and so you don't embarrass yourself, the term "wife swapping" is considered completely archaic), is prolific and encompasses a wide range of social activities that include, but are not limited to sex. Swingers eat, drink, play tennis, are bisexual; some are simply exhibitionists, some are voyeurs who only watch but don't engage, some may enjoy threesomes, others limit their sexual activities to oral sex. Swinging is considered to be a "fun" activity; swingers refer to sex as "play," and their sex partners as "playmates."

In the dark ages before the Internet, swinging lifestyle magazines such as the now defunct "Partner," were just about the only place where people with the same sexual interest could find each other. Today the web is where it's at to peruse swinging personal ads and make contacts.

Another way to hook up with other swingers is to find them in your community. It's dicey how you would approach a likely candidate, but not impossible. A simple rule of thumb is that a man should always approach another man; a woman another woman. Over beers or cocktails just very casually mention, "My wife and I are thinking of getting into swinging. Know anyone who's into that?" Make it sound like you're asking about tennis courts. Doubles, actually. Very likely, the other person will think you're joking and not take your question seriously. But for the one person who does, you'll get the info that you need, which puts you one step closer to making your debut into this very discreet society. At the end of the day, you'll be surprised how many people are into it.

PILLOW *talk*

I think men talk to women so they can *sleep* with them and women sleep with men so they can *talk* to them.

—Jay McInerney

no.
52

The act of urinating on your lover during sex is a fetish called a "golden shower."

This fetish is also known as urolagnia, urophilia, or undinism. Many people find the idea of a golden shower to be creepy. (In New Zealand, writing about it or talking about it on one's website is strictly illegal and punishable with a sentence of up to ten years in jail!) But enthusiasts of golden showers say they can be very erotic and thrilling. In fact, Havelock Ellis, the nineteenth-century physician who carved a respected academic career for himself by studying sex, had a personal fetish about urine. Ellis's own proclivity was watching girls urinate (mostly outdoors, quite often in ditches), but not to be urinated on.

The desire to be peed on can conjure up forbidden desires and fantasies, including elaborate scenarios involving hints of humiliation and debasement with a whiff of subjugation. Couples who try a golden shower usually want to change things up. They're merely trying things to do that are different, especially if they've been in a relationship for a long time. Sometimes you don't know what turns you on until you try it!

Despite popular belief, urine is not a foul substance as it exits the body. Clean, fresh urine is sterile. In the desert, it's even used as an astringent! In some Middle Eastern cultures, fresh urine from a healthy person is considered safe to drink.

PILLOW *talk*

Life
is the flower
of which
love
is the honey.

—Victor Hugo

53

High heels are sexy and fetishistic because they make the legs look so long and lean.

The high heel thrusts the weight on to the ball of the foot, which in turn pushes the calf muscle out, into a pronounced position so that it's bulging, the bulge being a subliminal erotic symbol, much like the bulge of an erection. High heels also make a woman taller, and appear stronger, more impressive, and dominating. Guys who enjoy being dominated prefer their women in heels. Other men just like the way heels make a woman look, which is to say, more erect, taller, more pulled together, polished. What man doesn't want to have an erect, striking woman on his arm? The red carpet effect is always spoiled by a lady wearing flats, not heels.

Foot worship, which is a specific fetish, is closely connected to adoration for high heels and boots with stiletto heels. An enormous culture of foot fetishism worldwide is devoted to various forms of foot and high heel fetishes. Several adult marketed video companies specialize in videos of high-heeled women trampling men prone on the floor, foot worship (the man at the high heeled woman's feet, bowing to kiss them) and sex involving the feet and toes.

A less dramatic variation of this fetish is the ordinary woman's desire, sometimes compulsion, to have her feet always be perfectly nice, i.e. weekly appointments and rituals and devotions to pedicures and having the right toenail color at all times. Toe cleavage, cosmetic surgery to improve toe cleavage, costly delicate shoes that showcase the feet, all are culturally accepted modifications and versions of the sexy high heel fetish.

PILLOW *talk*

I am sensual and very **physical.** *I'm very erotic. But my sexuality exists on sort of a fantasy level.*

—Donna Summer

It's estimated that fewer than 1 percent of the men in the world can successfully suck or lick their own penis.

Ron Jeremy, the fat, Jewish, dark, hairy guy from Queens, alternatively known as the Hedgehog, not only has a sizeable member, long and thick as a baby's forearm, but he can do tricks with it. Since the death of John Holmes, Ron Jeremy is ranked as America's Number One porn star. Not merely a sex star, but a live carnival side-show attraction, Jeremy's main claim to fame was laid not just by the size of his tool, but by his ability to suck it. He has demonstrated his unique, freaky, and undeniably comical technique to the world again and again in countless X-rated films.

Public auto-fellatio is a stunt, and Ron Jeremy, who holds a master's degree in Education and a BA in theater, early on began honing his circus-maximus style off the X-rated screen. He has appeared as himself on *The Weakest Link*, and has done cameos in legit movies and emcees at comedy clubs and celebrity roasts. His mainstream popularity continues to grow as he personally grows balder and older. In 2006 he published a book, "The Hardest Working Man in Show Business," which became a *New York Times* bestseller. And he continues to appear in adult films, claiming he'll stop when he "wakes up one morning and finds his dick on the pillow." But not since the 1970s has he ever sucked his own penis.

Few men have the flexibility and/or penis length to auto-fellate themselves. If you think you might be a candidate to join this fraternity, understand it's all about flexibility. Increased flexibility can be achieved by gravity-assisted positions or from being a diligent yoga student, gymnast, or amateur contortionist. Craig Bartle, an American biologist, estimated that less than 1 percent of the men in the world can successfully suck or lick their own dick.

PILLOW *talk*

I think **anything** *that has to do with sexuality makes people* **very** *interested.*

—Catharine Deneuve

no.
55

A *pro domme* is commonly addressed as "Mistress," "Ma'am," or "Maitresse."

A *pro domme*, that is a professional dominatrix, is a woman who has made a career out of pushing men around, telling them what to do, when to do it, when to speak, what to say, making them clean the toilet and getting well paid for it. A pro domme is also a woman who takes the dominant role in bondage and discipline, working with clients who think of themselves as submissives. The common form of address to such a person is "Mistress," "Ma'am," or "Maitresse." A dominatrix doesn't necessarily dominate a male partner. She can also work with female submissives.

Some dommes have personal slaves who do their housework, the grocery shopping, attend to errands. These are not paying clients. A slave in this relationship has no rights or limits. Dominatrixes very rarely have sexual contact with paying clients, which is why pro dommes are not prostitutes. They may have sex with a devoted slave.

Mistress Marina Black, a strict dominant sadist and a pro domme, calls herself a magician. "A dominatrix shapes reality," she said. "She makes fantasy a reality." Sandra Chemero, the former Bedford Hills Dominatrix, calls her work "role play," and beat a prostitution charge in that community. She told a reporter for a local newspaper that most of her clients were wealthy married couples and her job was to teach the wife how to be more dominant. By definition, a dominatrix is not a prostitute because she does not have sex for money.

There is also the whole question, are you a top or a bottom? Tops are, surprise, surprise, dominants, as they are "on top," literally. The top is generally perceived to be the aggressor or at least the leader in the equation. The top is the person in control, the one who determines what and how it will happen, according to the top's preferences. Bottoms, by definition, are submissive, the receiver, the more passive party. But don't let the labels fool you. It's not always obvious in a sexual relationship where the power lies.

PILLOW *talk*

It's my experience that the fluidity of sexuality with younger people is more accepted.

–Josh Schwartz

56

Pony play is neither child's play nor for the faint of heart!

Pony play is a game a client plays with a dominatrix that involves the client (usually male) getting on all fours on the carpet and the dominatrix mounting his back and riding him around the room, as though he were a pony. Sometimes called petplay or ponyism, pony play is a form of sexual role play where one or more of the participants takes on the role of an animal, including the animal's appropriate mannerisms and behaviors. That means the person playing the pony will be whinnying, neighing, bucking, pawing, shaking his head up and down, in other words, anything that simulates equine behavior.

The rider may take on the role of trainer, caretaker—or breeding partner. Sometimes elements of the slave/master dynamic may be involved. To get the most out of a pony play experience, the person taking the role of the pony should wear something that is like a bridle or a bit in his mouth. There should be some form of reins. A belt will serve these dual purposes in a pinch. Avid fans of pony play visit websites that specialize in play equipment, well worth the expense if you crave authenticity in your mildly foolish endeavors. Modified horse tack, masks, and prosthetic devices such as binding of the forearms or the calves to simulate horse bandages can be improvised.

Pony play is sometimes called "The Aristotelian Perversion," a nod to the ancient legend that Aristotle enjoyed a fetishistic penchant to be ridden like a horse. Please note that the human back is not strong enough to take the weight of another adult without risk of injury, so the riding is usually symbolic, with the "rider" handling most of their weight on his or her own legs. In 2003, a documentary film called "Pony Passion" was produced by a British pony play club depicting their club's activities, and in 2005, *Born in a Barn* was filmed, showing the lives and proclivities of pony play fanatics. Madonna and her backup dancers pretended to be engaging in pony play activities on stage during her 2006 tour.

Sexuality is the lyricism of the masses.

–Charles Baudelaire

Alfred Binet, who is better known for inventing the IQ test, also was the first to give a clinical name to sexual fetishism.

Richard von Krafft-Ebing, Alfred Binet, Viktor Frankl, Magnus Hirschfeld, and Donald Winnicut are all either psychiatrists, psychologists, or sexologists who studied erotic fetishism. Alfred Binet, who is better known for inventing the IQ test, also was the first to give a clinical name to erotic or sexual fetishism, calling it paraphilia. Binet recognized that rather than seek treatment for their obsession, many people choose to embrace their fetish. Frankl took an existential approach and influenced the view that fetishes have complex personal meanings beyond the categories of psychoanalytical treatment. Krafft-Ebing recognized the wide variety of fetishes, but could never properly explain or understand why some fetishes last a lifetime for a person, while others fade and disappear. (An example of this would be a long-held fetish for blonds that disappears when one marries a redhead.) Magnus proposed the theory of partial attractiveness, where in his theory sexual attraction to one person had not to do so much with the whole person, but a fetish for one or more of their features. He believed that everyone had special interests and engaged in healthy sorts of fetishes, such as a love for women with big boobs. Winnicut's theories revolve around transitional objects and phenomena; in his view, a fetish for cuddly toys and juvenile actions (this would include bathroom-oriented fetishes) comes out of the person's earliest childhood sexual associations.

Pursuit and seduction are the essence of sexuality. It's part of the sizzle.

—Camille Paglia

Infantilism is a fetish in which an adult gets hot when treated as an infant.

This means wearing diapers, wanting to be washed and pow-dered, dressed in (very large) plastic pants and baby clothes, talked to in baby talk, possibly wanting to be breastfed! Dozens of websites are devoted to adult babies and persons with a dia-per fetish. True infantilism is not a fetish per se; it's an individual who has been marked by regressive dependencies. Psychologists and mental health professionals say this person is usually isolated and alone and believes there is no one in the world like him or her. They usually keep their regression secret from other people. They may secretly wear dia-pers, suck on pacifiers, have a baby blanket, drink from a bottle.

The infantilism fetish is clinically known as paraphilia infantilism, characterized by a person, usually an adult male, who wears diapers as part of his foreplay habit and who wants his woman to treat him as though he were a toddler or an infant. A person who engages in infantilistic play is called an adult baby or AB.

There are categories within categories regarding adult babies or ABs. One in three ABs is also a diaper lover (DL) and these folks are collectively called AB/DLs. The majority of AB/DLs are heterosexual males. Another category is a sissy baby, usually a male AB/DL who throws a little gender play into his infantilism mix. This person might be a cross dresser who wants to wear little girl clothes or maybe a pink diaper cloth! An AB/DL masochist is someone who might want to be cross dressed by force.

Infantilism is viewed by some mental health professionals as a relief from stress. Obviously they're not dangerous! They just have a deep-seated desire to be helpless and irresponsible because babies are not held responsible for anything, and it's not their fault when they crap or wet their pants!

**P**ILLOW *talk*

Understand that sexuality is as wide as the sea.

–Derek Jarman

Key parties are parties where you go home with somebody else's spouse!

Key parties were hugely popular in the early 1970s when swinging was the racy pastime of people living in the suburbs. The typical key party was held at a well-to-do suburban home on a Friday night. It could never be on a Saturday because who could wake up in a strange house and then have to go to church?

During the party, guests mingled, drinking daiquiris and Tom Collinses, flirting and chatting and talking about any old thing. At some mysterious ill-defined point during the party, husbands dropped their key ring (house key, no car key attached) into a large bowl prominently displayed on the dining room table or some other previously agreed upon spot. Near the end of the party, when everyone was sufficiently smashed, the hostess gathered everyone into the room with the bowl and invited the women to select a key ring. The idea was that you went home

PILLOW talk

It's
sexier
when a girl
is flirty but
she doesn't do
anything.

—Paris Hilton

with whoever's key you picked up. This practice inevitably led to arguments, sore feelings, and jealousy.

No one knows how many key party players wound up divorced. A great example of a key party in modern cinema is the key party scene in the film, *The Ice Storm*, a 1997 drama directed by Ang Lee based on the novel of the same name by Rick Moody. The film is about two dysfunctional Connecticut families who deal with alcohol, adultery, and sexual experimentation. One only hopes that in real life, key parties were more fun.

Group sex rarely occurs spontaneously, despite what you see in the movies.

Group sex requires a great deal of social sensitivity and etiquette, usually set forth by whomever masterminds the orgy. Most successful encounters involve specific will-do, won't-do rules that are spelled out well in advance of anyone taking their clothes off. In fact, most group sex sessions are planned weeks beforehand.

Depending on where the sex is scheduled, it could happen at someone's home, at a special on-premise swinger's club, or you could meet your orgy mates at an off-premise establishment where you'll talk first and have a few drinks before retiring to another location, usually a hotel room.

Another way group sex can happen, usually in the form of a three-way, is that you and your significant other agree that you're going to pick someone up and bring him home. Others may opt for a swingers'

PILLOW talk

Once the buttons are undone, you know how it'll all end. It's all in the game, there are no miracles.

—Gao Xingjian

weekend where like-minded couples are in attendance and all the logistics are worked out by the club or company sponsoring the retreat. Another option would be to take your time and scan the personal ads looking for just the right individual or couple with whom to have sex.

People who are casually dating also occasionally engage in group sex, which is basically friends with benefits squared or quadrupled. If you find yourself in a group situation but you can't bring yourself to engage in intimate acts, don't. But if possible, try to be tactful when you refuse; never be ungracious or insulting. You can always make it up to your partners later, with a nonsexual offering along the lines of a neck massage or whipping up breakfast.

Eliot Spitzer's prostitute girlfriend is a pop singer whose songs are featured on YouTube.

She wasn't Ashley Alexandra Dupre, aspiring pop singer, then. That girl was "Kristen," a $4,000-a-night call girl working for the Emperor's Club VIP, a house of prostitution. (Spitzer was known as Client No. 9.) According to published reports, federal agents had been wiretapping Spitzer for years, and it is estimated that he spent $80,000 on hookers, first as attorney general and then later as governor. The investigation that led to the governor's downfall had been sparked in the first place after the North Fork Bank reported suspicious transactions to the IRS as required by the Bank Secrecy Act.

On March 10, 2008, The *New York Times* broke the story online that Spitzer had arranged numerous meetings with the 5-foot, 5-inch, then 105-pound, call girl over a period of months, paying more than

PILLOW *talk*

The way you
make love
is the way
God will
be with you.

—Rumi

$15,000 for her services. Nobody really knows much about Ashley Alexandra Dupre, the real woman. She hasn't published her autobiography . . . yet. Most recently she is a pop singer whose songs, "What We Want," and "Move Your Body," can be seen and heard on YouTube. A photo exclusive of her lounging on the beach at the Jersey Shore in June 2008 in the company of Carolyn Capalbo, her mother, revealed the young woman has packed on a few pounds since her Spitzer days. She also added a new tattoo. On her lower belly is a butterfly and the Latin phrase, "tutela valui," which Latin scholars have opined means, "fair value."

no.

62

The late singer Marvin Gaye was truly in need of sexual healing.

Best known for his singles, "Sexual Healing" and "Let's Get It On," Marvin Gaye was allegedly addicted to sex. While hanging out with Gaye when he was living in Ostend, Belgium, his biographer, David Ritz, reportedly freaked out when he saw Gaye's enormous collection of S&M porn. Ritz declared, "Man, you need sexual healing," although sadly Gaye never chose to get it.

As Motown's top male artist in the 1960s, Gaye recorded hits including "How Sweet It Is to Be Loved by You" and "I Heard It Through the Grapevine," before being paired with the golden-voiced Tammi Terrell, the woman with whom Gaye produced a string of hits including "Ain't Nothing Like the Real Thing," and "Your Precious Love." During a performance, Terrell collapsed in Gaye's arms on stage in 1967 and was soon diagnosed with a brain tumor. She died three years later and afterwards Gaye went into seclusion for two years, emerging only to record "What's Going On," which became an antiwar anthem.

Marvin Gaye married twice, but neither relationship stuck, and Gaye sank deeper into depression. He became addicted to the works of French bondage cartoonist Georges Pichard, and, after leaving Belgium, isolated himself in his parents' house, a big mistake, because his father was a Pentecostal preacher. After threatening to commit suicide several times after bitter arguments with his dad, Gay senior (Marvin added an 'e' to their family name), shot and killed his son after arguing over some misplaced business documents. At the time of his death, Gaye and his current paramour, Lady Edith Foxwell, a doyenne of London café society, had been discussing marriage.

ILLOW
talk

When it comes to being a good lover, a guy has to ask a girl what she wants and be willing to give it to her.

—Jenna Jameson

The Happy Hooker once worked as a copywriter for ad agency J. Walter Thompson.

Dutch-born Xaviera Hollander is best known for her autobiographical story, *The Happy Hooker,* which was published in 1971. The book was an enormous and immediate hit, praised for its humor, honesty, and candor. Hollander, born in the Dutch East Indies to a Jewish father and French-German mother, was first a copywriter for J. Walter Thompson and then a secretary to the Dutch consul in the United States. To supplement her salary at the consulate, she began working as a call girl, making $1,000 a night.

In 1969, she borrowed $10,000 from one of her customers to purchase the client list of a retiring madam. Calling her new business the Vertical Whorehouse, Hollander began managing girls, customers, and all of the money, ratcheting herself up in her profession to become the city's most famous madam. While penning her famous advice column for *Penthouse* magazine, Hollander was investigated by the Knapp Commission, and shortly after was arrested for prostitution. She was forced to leave the United States.

In 2002 she published a sequel to her life story called, *Child No More: A Memoir.* Today she runs a bed and breakfast called Xaviera's Happy House in Amsterdam and another at her villa in Marbella, Spain. Still thriving, in Amsterdam in 2007 she married Philip de Haan, a Dutch man ten years her junior. Still writing, her topics these days are love and food.

PILLOW talk

I'd like to meet the man who **invented** *sex and see what he's working on now.*

—Unknown

Basketball hall of famer Wilt (the Stilt) Chamberlain was so large he had to have custom condoms made.

No drugstore sold any brand that could accommodate his massive size. The seven-foot-one-inch Chamberlain who weighed 250 pounds as a rookie and eventually over 300 pounds when he played center position with the Lakers, is widely perceived to be one of the greatest and most dominant players in the history of the NBA. Reputed to have been a big player between the sheets, Wilt told Howard Stern that he had made love to thousands of women and verified once and for all the rumors that his rubbers were custom made.

PILLOW
talk

Of all the sexual aberrations, chastity is the *strangest.*

–Anatole France

The term "sadism" is derived from the Marquis de Sade's name.

The true identity and name of the Marquis de Sade, alas, is a mystery that may never be solved. What is known is that the man known as the Marquis de Sade was born into a noble family in Paris, France, in 1740, and died imprisoned at Charenton in 1814 at the age of seventy-four.

By the time he was twenty-three, the Marquis had been discovered by his sisters and his mother to be heavily involved with prostitutes. Whatever it was he was doing with them was deemed by his family to be so horrifying and perverse that they had him imprisoned without a trial. He remained behind bars for fourteen years.

Upon his release, he became a revolutionary during the time of the Terror, narrowly missing losing his head to the guillotine several times. Although his listed occupations included noble, writer, poet, critic, and even at one point delegate to the National Convention, the Marquis's voluminous writings and diaries are considered to be exceedingly strange, even criminal, as his preferred subject matter ran to the brutal and fetishistic.

He led a wild and wicked life, having affairs with his wife's sister, his manservant, Latour, drugging prostitutes with Spanish Fly, holding young women for days at a time against their will as sex slaves. In 1801, Napoleon Bonaparte had him imprisoned for penning (anonymously) the erotic novels *Justine,* and *Juliet,* which are erotic bondage stories. Allegations that the Marquis attempted to seduce the young prisoners at the Sainte-Pelagie prison got him sent to the much harsher fortress, Bicetre.

The rowdy Marquis de Sade spent thirty-two years of his life in various jails and insane asylums, which is where he did most of his writing. The term "sadism" is derived from his name. Sadism is a form of satisfaction, often sexual, derived from inflicting harm or pain on another person.

PILLOW *talk*

Sex is as important as eating or drinking and we ought to allow the one appetite to be satisfied with as little restraint or false modesty as the other.

–Marquis de Sade

There once was a nation run by prostitutes!

The so-called "Rule of the Harlots" was a period that took place during the first half of the tenth century. It began with the installation of Pope Sergius III in A.D. 904 This strange period in the history of the Papacy lasted for sixty years, ending only with the death of Pope John XII in 964. Some scholars describe it as ending about thirty years earlier, with the reign of Pope John XI in 935.

"The Rule of the Harlots," sometimes called a pornocracy, was a nation of prostitutes and a government dominated by them. It all revolved around a Roman woman called Marozia or Mariuccia, who was given the title of senatrix and patricia of Rome by Pope John X. Up until that point, there were no women in the Roman senate. Marozia was the daughter of the Roman consul Theophylact, Count of Tusculum and of Theodora, a real mover and shaker in Rome, a woman characterized later by historians as a "shameless whore." By many lights, it was Theodora herself who really controlled both the city of Rome and the Papacy.

Edward Gibbon, the British historian and member of Parliament whose most important work, *The History of the Decline and Fall of the Roman Empire*, was published between 1776 and 1788, wrote rather entertainingly about Marozia and Theodora and their influence in their world. Mother and daughter bulldozed and bullied the Church and the government through their beauty and their wealth. Their amorous and political intrigues were renowned. Only their most adored and virile lovers were rewarded with Roman money and swag, and the two women's powerful associations with the Church led to a belief that there was indeed once a female pope.

The term "pornocracy," is associated with the effective rule of Rome of Theodora and her daughter Marozia through male surrogates. The Papess, which was a tarot card used in France by the people of Marseilles in the eighteenth century, in fact depicts a female pope.

Scholars know that during the first century, the popes were strongly influenced by powerful and aristocratic families such as Theophylact's and his kin. Powerful women who weren't prostitutes also made major contributions and enjoyed considerable influence on the Church and the government. It is believed that Marozia was the concubine of Pope Sergius III and the mother of Pope John XI. She was accused of arranging the murder of Pope John X (originally put up for the office by none other than her mother Theodora) in order to elevate her own favorite.

Throughout the "Rule of the Harlots," Pope John XII (955–963), who was a grandson of Marozia, was guilty of every lewd crime. He violated widows and virgins, took up with his father's mistress, and turned the Papal Palace into a brothel. Pope John XII met his end when he was killed while caught in the act of adultery by the woman's enraged husband.

Sex was never as neat as the movies made it. Real sex was messy. Good sex was messier.

—Laurell K. Hamilton

There's no real correlation between the size of a man's hands and his penis size.

Although folklore abounds comparing the size of a man's hands, his feet, the length of his nose, and his fingers to, uh, more private parts of his physique, there is nothing at all to any of these theories. Many men who have big hands and feet do indeed have large members, but it's just as likely that a man with a big penis has small hands. Or vice versa.

The results of a study of 104 men with foot sizes 8 through 13 surveyed and examined at St. Mary's Hospital and University College Hospital in London published in the *British Journal of Urology International* reported that there is no link between foot size and penis thickness or length, stating there is no medical evidence to support this widespread, long-held foot-penis size theory.

Even so, human beings want to believe. We want to see patterns even where none exist to assume the human body was built on a precise scale. But Mother Nature defied this notion by coming up with random patterns. The only halfway reliable way to gauge a guy's penis size before you've felt or seen it is to listen closely to what the guy says about it. For example, guys who immediately own up to their small penises often really have little ones. And many guys who brag about their big cock and strut around as God's gift are often well-endowed. (Unfortunately, these big-cock guys often have enormous egos; in which case, you'd be better off dating the guy with the small penis who has a dexterous tongue!)

PILLOW talk

A man might forget where he parks or where he lives, but he **never** *forgets oral sex, no matter how bad it is.*

—Barbara Bush

In 90 percent of cases, the body rids itself of HPV through its immune system within a few years of getting infected.

The human papillomavirus, HPV as it is called, is the most common sexually transmitted infection or STD. It starts in the mucous membranes and the skin and is so capable of mutation that it can become one of forty known strains that infect men and women. The penis, the vulva, the anus, the lining of the vagina, the cervix, and the rectum can all be infected, and because it's painless, most people don't even know they're infected. The types of HPV that cause genital warts are not the same as the types that cause cancer. Although some HPVs are known to be precancerous in disposition, in 90 percent of cases the body rids itself of the infection through its immune system within a couple of years.

Genital HPVs are mostly passed from one person to another during vaginal or anal sex. Rarely, although it is possible, a pregnant woman can pass her HPV on to her baby during a vaginal delivery. In these cases, the baby may develop warts on its throat or voice box. This condition is known as recurrent respiratory papillomatosis, or RRP.

HPVs can be avoided now through a vaccine. Chances are you've seen the ads on TV. This vaccine is somewhat controversial, but recommended for girls and women between the ages of eleven and twenty-six to help them avoid contracting the four types of HPV known to cause genital warts and cervical cancer. Currently there is no vaccine licensed to prevent HPV-related diseases in men.

PILLOW *talk*

Sex

is a

shortcut

to

everything.

—Anne Cumming

no.
69

A happy sexual relationship gets imprinted into cell memory, which makes a great lover, who just happens to be an ex, hard to forget.

So . . . could you, should you, do it one last time? Having sex with your ex is so tempting. There's the knowledge of the flesh, the remembered orgasms, the practiced rhythm a couple establishes when they've been getting physical for a long time. New bodies are fun, but there's something about making it with an old boyfriend or girlfriend that sends a thrill down everybody's spine.

Sex with your ex is supposed to be forbidden, but ex-couples do it all the time. An incredibly large number of people who have been divorced from each other for years still will occasionally take a roll in the hay if opportunity knocks and the chance is given. The sex can take place years after the break-up. It's funny how many divorced parents whose child is graduating from college wind up spending the night together if they've come a long distance and find themselves in the same hotel bar hours after the ceremony's over.

Does it hurt anyone when a couple who are exed have sex? Depends . . . on a few factors.

Sex isn't what usually broke a couple up, and if the sex was exceptional between them, they don't forget it. The body (and the brain) remember outstanding sex and it's not unusual to find yourself masturbating or in the middle of a female wet dream dreaming about sex with an ex. A happy sexual relationship gets imprinted into cell memory, making a great lover, who just happens to be a former lover, hard to forget. So when you happen to see that person again, even if you parted on bad terms and basically despise each other, there's still that little jolt to the genitals when you see him. A person can turn you on even if they are your enemy. Sometimes *because* they are your enemy!

Sex with your ex can be complicated, but it also can be hot fun. Sex with your ex is almost always thrilling, exciting, exhilarating, and delicious. (It can also be a major bummer if one of you won't stop crying.) Half the reason for the heat is the forbiddenness, the sensation that you've broken some set-in-stone social law. The other half of the excitement is based purely on physical sensation. Nobody knows your body like the person you used to make love to. That person is fully alert and aware of how you respond to certain stimuli (like a gifted, uber-talented tongue), and what most turns you on.

Familiarity, by the way, is totally underrated as an aphrodisiac. In some ways, sex with your ex is exactly like comfort food. In times of stress you crave it. It's the nourishment you reach for when you're stressed or depressed or freaked out. At the end of the day, sex with your ex, just like comfort food, is delicious and probably bad for you, but it feels so good going down.

Be aware, however, that sex with your ex can also spark a storm. Instead of your mutually delirious heart-stopping orgasms, there's always the potential for tears, shouting, and a volley of recriminations. Be prepared that so much energy can release all kinds of emotions. The very volatile nature of having sex with your ex can result in damage and bloodshed!

One of the things you should ask yourself before mindlessly hopping in the sack with the person you used to be with is, "Are you really over?"

Have a real conversation with yourself on this one. People often have sex with their ex because they're really not done with them, or they want to see if there's still a flame. They're on the lookout for any spark that might catch and rekindle the relationship. Broken-up couples do get back together all the time (before tying the knot, most couples break up at least twice, the course of true love being rocky and circuitous), so if you think you might/could get back together, give sex a chance. If it's still great after all you've been through, maybe you should be together . . . or just get together once in a while to have sex. The emotional/psychological part of the relationship might truly be over, but that doesn't necessarily mean that your sex relationship can't continue.

Is sex with your ex ever convenience sex? Yes. Is that something that you want or need? No answer is wrong here as long as you're honest with yourself . . . and your ex. If you're not seeing anybody and neither is your ex and you're both horny, consenting adults, is it wrong? No, it is not.

PILLOW *talk*

The sexual drive is nothing but the motor memory of **previously** *remembered pleasure.*

—Wilhelm Reich

no.
70

A long penis may be an advantage for hitting a woman's G spot.

There is no proof, medical or scientific, that the guy carrying more weight in his pants can better satisfy a woman in bed. A guy with no penis at all can bring any woman to orgasm with his tongue. Or his fingers. Or both. That said, there are advantages to having a large penis, both lengthwise as well as width.

The guy who is wide takes up more overall volume inside the vaginal shaft, the resulting feeling of fullness meaning that his partner can enjoy feeling completely filled. This is especially appealing to women who have delivered a large number of children and whose vaginas are a bit stretched out. In that case, having a fatty is a boost and a benefit for both parties, as no guy likes to feel like there's a lot of extra room to fill down there. A long penis may be an advantage for hitting a woman's G spot, if hers is situated in a slightly lower position in her lower abdomen. For the record, a woman's G spot is not always in exactly the same place. Just because you found the G spot on your former girlfriend doesn't mean you'll automatically be able to place your finger—or the tip of your penis—on it with your next partner. Having a long penis that presses up against the woman's cervix is both a blessing and a curse, depending on the inner dimensions of your partner. Some women have short vaginal passages while others have a longer road that might even have a slight twist or bend to it.

While the right-sized penis in the ideally matched up pussy is nothing short of heavenly bliss, the wrong-sized penis trying to work its way into a too short, too narrow chute can result in painful, definitely unsatisfying, congress for both partners.

PILLOW *talk*

Sex is like **snow**, *you never know how many inches you're going to get or how long it will last.*

—Unknown

Post-sex rashiness and redness can last for up to an hour.

That's the post-coital flush. Most women after (and sometimes during) the act of love, are surprised to see a measle-like flush that extends over their chests and necks after intercourse. What's the cause? This all over the chest and neck blush is caused by sexual excitement. It's perfectly natural and in fact is a sign of good sexual health. Only about 50 percent of women in menopause experience it due to the decrease in hormones. (Menopausal women are more likely to have a hot flash than a hot flush.) Only time makes the livid hue go away, which makes it tricky to have sex on your lunch hour and not have everyone in the office know about it.

PILLOW *talk*

**Part of the sexual
revolution is bringing
rationality to sexuality
—because when
you don't embrace
sexuality in a
normal way, you get
the twisted kinds . . .**

—Hugh Hefner

Jan Vinzenz Krause, a thirty-something German entrepreneur, says that condoms should be more like shoes.

Acknowledging the need for different sizes for different members, this German sex-health educator has designed a prototype for a custom-fit spray-on condom made out of liquid latex. Still in the testing phase, the invention has been met with mixed reviews, mostly because the contraption hisses as it sprays, which can kill the mood. Another downfall is its impracticality—liquid latex takes about three minutes to set. Until a faster-drying latex is available, it's unlikely this novel condom will get off the ground. In the meantime, Krause is working on a line of condoms that come in six sizes, instead of one or two. Those will be released in Europe before making their way to the States, although for the time being the new line will be sold online. According to Krause, this is to take away the awkwardness of the drugstore transaction for guys who are very small—or very big!

PILLOW *talk*

Condoms should be
marked in 3 sizes:
jumbo, colossal,
and super colossal,
so that men do not
have to go in and
ask for the small.

—Barbara Seaman

Boogie Nights director Paul Thomas Anderson was, for a time, fascinated with pornography personalities.

Written, co-produced, and directed by Paul Thomas Anderson, *Boogie Nights*, a film about the porn industry during its golden age of the late 1970s and early 1980s, won a Golden Globe award. Starring Mark Wahlberg, Burt Reynolds, William H. Macy, Julianne Moore, Don Cheadle, John C. Reilly, Philip Seymour Hoffman, and Heather Graham, the film depicted the rise and fall of a fictional porn star called Dirk Diggler and how cocaine and crystal meth triggered his impotence and paranoia. The director, Paul Thomas Anderson, was for a time fascinated with pornography and the personalities and foibles of porn stars and people connected to the porn business. Anderson very seriously researched everything he could about the industry and became a pain in the ass to studio execs at New Line because he refused to cut what he'd shot, or turn the film into a light nostalgic comedy.

What was released into theaters was a complex, dark drama, over three hours long. Critics loved it and showered it with praise. *Boogie Nights* eventually grossed $43,101,594 internationally. The film was nominated for three Oscars although it didn't win. While *Boogie Nights* does have its humorous moments, mainly it focuses on drug use and despair and very specifically depicts how the Mafia got into the adult film business and took it over from its kinder, more joyful roots. All the events in the film take place between 1977 and 1984. Actual porn stars Veronica Hart, Little Cinderella, Summer Cummings, Skye Blue, Joe Sausage, and Tony Tedeschi have bit parts in the film.

PILLOW *talk*

At the **heart** *of pornography is sexuality* **haunted** *by its own disappearance.*

—Jean Baudrillard

74

When Nelson Rockefeller died, he was in bed with someone other than his wife.

Nelson Aldrich Rockefeller was the forty-first vice president of the United States, the forty-ninth governor of New York, a philanthropist, a businessman, and a descendent of one of America's wealthiest families. Regarded as a liberal Republican, Rockefeller was responsible for creating New York State's stringent laws against drug users, which remain among the toughest in the United States. It was Rockefeller who ordered 1,000 National Guardsman and New York State Troopers into Attica prison after four days of rioting, after which forty people died.

In his spare time, he busied himself with massive building contracts and was the driving force behind New York State's university system, which became the largest system of higher education in the nation. He was interested in conservation, crime, and absolutely in sex. While married to Margaretta "Happy" Rockefeller, Nelson suffered a fatal heart attack in his West 54th Street Manhattan townhouse in the company of his twenty-six–year-old aide, Megan Marshack. Marshack phoned her pal, news reporter Ponchitta Pierce, to come to the townhouse and it was Pierce who phoned for an ambulance. While the press wildly speculated about what was going on between Rockefeller and Marshack, the family never commented. The most they ever would say was that Rockefeller was working on a book about his art collection.

PILLOW *talk*

Seduction is always more singular and sublime than **sex** *and it commands the higher price.*

—Jean Baudrillard

A Strap-On Sally can help you change things up in the bedroom.

A Strap-On Sally is a dildo, an artificial penis, that can be strapped onto your body during sex so that you can penetrate your partner. When gay guys use them, they're repackaged as Strap-On Jacks. Strap-On Sallies that are made from a variety of man-made materials, usually plastic or latex, are used primarily, although not exclusively, by lesbians who crave more than finger and tongue or fisting action during intercourse.

Men who suffer from severe erectile dysfunction sometimes use them to satisfy their wives, and women whose male partners desire anal penetration will strap one on, so to speak, in order to enter their partners from behind. Strap-On Sallies come in all shapes and sizes and different price ranges, too, depending not just on how many inches you want and what a size queen you are, but the quality of the strapping material, too.

PILLOW *talk*

Having sex is like playing bridge. If you don't have a good partner, you'd better have a good hand.

—Woody Allen

76

You can preserve your own penis by creating a mold for a dildo!

A dozen or so sites on the web pledge and promise that you can make your own dildo, using your own equipment. Or you can shop directly online for porn star molds that come with their own kits to make at home. The Clone-a-Willy manufactured by Empire Labs is a kit that allows you to make a mold of your own penis. (Be patient—it could take a few tries!)

How does it work? The kit comes with a tube, some rubber mixtures, and a small vibrator. What happens is you cut the tube to fit the length of your erect penis (have on hand a stack of porn or a willing partner to help you stay hard) and then you pour in the fast-acting rubber compound. The compound hardens in about two minutes, forming the mold. Next you pour in the liquid latex, which takes twenty-four hours to harden. When it's hardened, you pull the product out of the mold and have a perfect replica of your penis. What you do with it next is your own business!

PILLOW *talk*

The omnipresent
process of sex, as it is
woven into the whole
texture of a man's or
woman's body, is the
pattern of all the
process of all our life.

—Havelock Ellis

no.
77

Lube jobs make sex more slippery and fun!

Everybody and anybody and can benefit from using lubricants. Lubrication makes everything slide and glide and gets big things into small places. Lubes combat vaginal dryness and should always be used with sex toys and for exploring anal sex. Certain orifices don't naturally make any lube of their own (the anus immediately springs to mind) and for any object to enter such a space, lubrication is a necessity. Lubes also make sex more enjoyable and in some cases, make it last longer.

Some of the most popular lubes on the market are KY jelly, baby oil, and Vaseline, although baby oil and Vaseline should not be used in conjunction with latex objects such as diaphrams and condoms because they erode the latex and compromise their safety. Commercial lubes are either made of silicone or they're water based. Water-based lubes have the advantage of flushing out of the body more easily and they are less expensive; silicone-based lubes never dry up or evaporate on the skin, but to get them off your skin requires soap and water. Thicker lubricants are better for anal sex and to use with toys. Some people are allergic to lubricants. The ingredient many people are allergic to is paraben preservative. If you suspect you might have an allergy, be sure to check the label of any product closely before you buy.

PILLOW *talk*

Sex . . . or lack thereof . . . is at the center of everyone's identity, and once you've cracked someone's desires, you understand them in full.

—Arianne Cohen

no.
78

Sex slings are not *just* for people who are into bondage. . . .

Anybody can use a sex sling, which is not so much a toy as a device. Traditionally the slings, which were tethered to the ceiling, were used by gay men to support one person while he was being "done." Hetero couples use slings now too, to enhance their sexual pleasure. Slings allow the wearer to adjust straps to afford deeper penetration and to leave the hands free for other pleasures. Most slings made today consist of a neck pillow that attaches to two buckles that are on a sturdy nylon strap, each of which attaches to an ankle cuff. The cushion ideally doesn't chafe the skin and the buckles should release quickly to allow the wearer confidence as well as flexibility. Slings take the pressure off the back and legs, which makes them ideal for couples who have weight or back problems.

PILLOW *talk*

Sex is emotion

in motion.

—Mae West

Most women are indeed hornier when they're fertile.

Makes sense, right? This is nature's way of telling them that their body is ready to get pregnant. The ovulation stimulates the hormones and triggers sexual excitement. Also many women find that their nipples are more sensitive and they're more responsive to touch while they're ovulating. During ovulation, when the female body is most receptive to the man's seed, the woman's basal body temp rises, making her literally hotter. Biologically speaking, most women feel that their sex drive kicks into high gear during ovulation at mid-cycle, or about fourteen days before they're due to get their next period. Surges in estrogen plus added testosterone that comes with ovulation might explain why the libido is heightened.

If you look at it in terms of evolution, it makes a lot of sense. Nature designed the female body for reproduction, so if she grabs you and wants to make love and it's her fertile time of the month, go for it. She could be an animal in the sack! Just don't get carried away by her ardor and forget about birth control unless you want to make a baby.

G spot finders are like a GPS system to a woman's No. 1 pleasure zone.

A dozen varieties or more are on the market that claim or promise that they will locate a woman's G spot, lickety-split. While many men are still in the dark on how to find their partner's *other* magic button, these engaging contraptions promise to bring pleasure to the user with minimal effort! Many women consider these tools to be basically another kind of personal massager with an attached wand that goes up high enough into the vagina to access the G spot.

New enhancements to G-spot finding equipment are G spot straps that allow for deeper penetration. With pressure controlled by the man from loops on either side, he can pull the strap tight to compress the vaginal canal, resulting in a more profound orgasm for her. Popular brands are Hitachi Magic Wand with Jelly Wand attachment, the G Force, and the G Spot Angler.

Expect to pay around $60 for a good piece of equipment, and don't forget to invest in a $15 bottle of Before & After Toy Cleaner.

PILLOW *talk*

I really

enjoy

having sex,

and that's

offensive

to some people.

—Megan Fox

81

The rectum is a highly sensitive orifice, chock full of nerve endings.

Butt plugs are used by both men and women to stimulate and tickle and tease that *other* orifice: the rectum. The rectum, you may not be aware, is a highly sensitive orifice, chock full of nerve endings. Butt plugs come in a variety of sizes, shapes, and technologies. There are simple plugs that are used to simulate anal penetration and then there are vibrating models that penetrate and massage.

Butt plugs look a lot like dildoes but are smaller and tend to have a flared edge so they don't get lost or stuck up inside someone's anus. Some look like penises, some are ribbed or wavy. They can be made of latex, silicone, glass, stone, even wood or metal. Silicone has it over many other materials as boiling it in water can clean it. It's wise to use a butt plug with a condom to avoid fecal mess. Butt plugs should not be shared with other people as they can transfer HIV. They tend to be a bit tricky to remove as the sphincter muscle clasps hard around them. Whether you're putting it in or taking it out, be sure to use a lot of lube!

ILLOW
talk

Sexual

energy

really

does

drive me. . . .

—Kate Hudson

A merkin is a wig for your pubic area.

Originally worn by prostitutes who shaved off their pubic hair in an effort to disguise the fact that they had lice, or to cover up the marks left behind from syphilis, merkins have been in existence in one form or another since the fifteenth century. Merkins were originally fashioned of either human or animal hair. Today they are primarily worn as a sexual costume or for fetish purposes. The designer Gianni Versace used merkins in 1992 as costume on the catwalk.

Modern merkins are usually pretty, sequin-covered decorative pubic garments worn by showgirls and burlesque queens, who further accessorize their otherwise naked bodies by wearing pasties or tassels on their breasts to hide their nipples. Merkins are affixed to the body either with spirit gum or by sewing them on to a transparent g-string.

Because merkins are so fully associated with disguise, the word also has another meaning in gay slang to describe a man who acts like a date or even marries a woman who is a lesbian in order to make her appear in public as a heterosexual. In this case, the merkin is the equivalent of a beard, which is a woman who dates or marries a gay man so that people will think he's heterosexual.

The word merkin as an inside joke is always good for a laugh, which is why it appears so often in plays, movies, and TV shows. The word merkin has appeared in episodes of *The Simpsons, Family Guy,* and *The L Word.* Pearl Jam and Neil Young released an album together called *Merkin Ball.* Thomas Pynchon wrote about merkins in *Gravity's Rainbow.* And Merkin is the name of a character in the popular Sandman comic books.

Modern merkins are usually decorated with sequins and feathers. If you've gone overboard with the Brazilian waxing, will wearing a merkin keep your pubic area warm? Could be, but investing in fur underpants would be wiser.

PILLOW *talk*

Golf is a sex game.

The goal is to get

the ball in the hole.

—Justin Timberlake

Twenty minutes is the maximum time a cock ring should be left on.

Cock rings, sometimes called penis rings, are used to enhance sexual pleasure. The ring binds the penis and testicles, trapping blood in the penis, which leads to greater sensation, more engorgement, and a firmer erection. Cock rings come in many styles and colors (although the preferred color is black). Some come in the basic strap style, while others have extras that actually vibrate the clitoris during hetero intercourse. Cock rings can be put on at any point during an erection.

Twenty minutes is the maximum time one should be left on; anything more can bruise the penis or damage the capillaries. Their use is not recommended for anyone with vascular disease, diabetes, or nerve damage. If you feel discomfort wearing one at any time, take it right off! Cock rings that are too tight can cause the medical emergency of priapism, which can cause penile gangrene. Falling asleep wearing one can pose a real problem of permanent nerve damage.

To use a cock ring, strap it around the base of the penis and behind the testicles. A man may choose to use a cock ring because he has erectile dysfunction. A cock ring will help him stay hard. Some men just like them as a sex toy because of the sensation of tightness and extra hardness. Vibrating rings, sometimes called "Dolphins" in online sex toy catalogs, use two removable vibrators that stimulate the anus or the perineum as well as the clitoris of the partner. Gay men are major purchasers of cock rings as they make the penis thicker and more engorged and therefore more visually stimulating to a partner. Some underwear marketed to men includes a pouch with an internal fabric elastic cock ring or "c" ring that encircles the penis. This type of pouch allows the wearer to don a thong or go "backless."

A cock ring is not to be confused with an Arab Strap, which is a device made of leather and a metal ring that is placed around the penis and testicles. This is a bondage type of sex toy, so named because it pays homage to the restraining devices used long ago for mating Arabian horses in the desert.

PILLOW *talk*

The human spirit sublimates the impulses it thwarts; a healthy sex life mitigates the lust for other sports.

—Piet Hein

Sex is good for your skin.

There is a connection between sex and your complexion, the connection being good sex, good skin. In direct contradiction to that old saw that masturbation will result in pimples, a cheap ploy to make young people feel bad about self-pleasuring that reached its apex in the straight-laced 1950s, good sex means good skin. Bedroom action boosts a flagging complexion, giving a nice rosy glow to the skin. Screen legend Joan Crawford once boasted to celebrity magazines that she needed regular sex for her skin, although she preferred "doing it" for love.

That flush of love aside, there is a real physiological explanation as to why sex is good for your skin. When the body becomes heated, harmful toxins are expelled and flushed from the system. Also the circulatory burst that accompanies orgasm means that the heart rate increases and that more blood is pumped throughout the body, especially to the face.

(That's why when you have an orgasm, you tend to turn quite pink.) During exuberant, energetic sex, plumping elastin fibers and collagen (the kind you pay a lot for at the cosmetic counter or the drugstore) are pumped straight to the face.

Another beneficial element is that endorphins are released during sex, endorphins being those sexy hormones that affect the brain like morphine. What this means is that in addition to looking good, you're feeling good, and that has a positive effect on your complexion.

Women do not enjoy, however, the scrubbed, burned, rubbed raw face that can last for hours after making love. The culprit here is a partner who hasn't made proper use of his razor! A rough male beard, especially that sexy, permanent 5-o'clock shadow carefully cultivated by many men, is very taxing on feminine facial skin and the tender insides of her thighs. Men, absolutely do shave!

PILLOW talk

I shave and groom
my private areas. It's
a better presentation
for me. If men require
women to go through
the pain, we should
return the favor.

—P. Diddy

Move over, Mrs. Robinson, cougars and pumas are on the loose!

"Milf" is an acronym for "Mother I'd Like to Fuck." Teenage boys are most interested in MILF's and for good reason. These ladies are hot mamas! Plus when you're young and inexperienced, a really great-looking mom in her forties is great fodder for fantasy. To be sure, she can teach you some things.

That said, the next step up from a MILF is a cougar. A cougar is a hot-looking, hot- acting, just plain hot woman in her late forties or older who is attracted to much younger guys. Like twenty or more years younger. If you're a young guy and you happen to get hooked up with a cougar, you're in real luck. You're in store for a big treat and quite the sexual education. Just remember that big cats have big claws . . . watch out that when she's done playing she doesn't scratch you—or eat you.

PILLOW
talk

Scratch most feminists and **underneath** *there is a woman who longs to be a sex object, the difference is that is not all she longs to be.*

—Betty Rollin

Pumas are the latest wild animal on the horizon. These are secure, thirty-something women who, because they are focused on their career and not interested in settling down, prefer shacking up with twenty-something guys because they are less hassle. (Seems like a great time to be a guy in your twenties!)

no.
86

Sex is more important than money for happiness.

There is solid evidence indicating that having an active sex life rates higher than having a lot of money on most peoples' happiness quotients. After studying the responses of 16,000 people who participated in the General Social Surveys of the United States conducted in the 1990s, economist David Blanchflower of Dartmouth College and Andrew Oswald of the University of Warwick in England concluded that sex is so important in personal happiness equations that they guesstimated that increasing intercourse from once a month to once a week would be the equivalent of getting an additional $50,000 a year.

Sex, they said, has a more profound effect on the happiness of highly educated people than on those who only finished high school. Homosexuals aren't necessarily happier than straight people, but they tend to have more sexual activity. Married people have more sex than those

PILLOW *talk*

Money,
it turned out, was
exactly like sex,
you thought of
nothing else if
you didn't have
it and thought
of other things if
you did.

—James Arthur Baldwin,
American playwright
and novelist

who are single, divorced, widowed, or separated. At the end of the day, the research concluded that having a lot of money might buy you more sexual partners, but not more sex.

If a guy's pupils are dilated, he's aroused.

Along with flared nostrils, slight sweating, and a suddenly hyperactive heartbeat, pupil dilation tells the true story of male desire. These four things are classic male involuntary physical responses to sexual arousal. Ever heard that old sixties song, "The Girl Can't Help It?" Well, no guy can help revealing his condition of arousal in the presence of a female who is adept at reading these bodily details. That's why it's so important to make a guy take his shades off. That's the only way to see him for what he is. His pupils are dilated? There are only a few explanations: it's bright outside, he's had one too many beers, or he's punch drunk for you!

PILLOW *talk*

Love is just a system for getting someone to call you darling after sex.

—Julian Barnes, British TV critic

Medical experts agree that if you want to get pregnant, the best position to take is . . . *any* position!

While some couples believe that their chances for conception are improved by the missionary position (man on top, woman on her back, legs raised), there is no scientific proof this position is more impregnating than any other. Other people think that the deeper penetration achieved by doing it doggy-style helps the sperm meet the egg. But that's not necessarily true either. What does count if babymaking is your goal is not position. To make conception more likely, have sex a day or two before you ovulate, and then again on the day of ovulation. Why does this work? Because sperm lives for two or three days, but the egg is only around for twelve to twenty-four hours. Having sex a day or two before ovulation and then again on the day of ovulation increases the likelihood that a healthy supply of sperm is waiting in the fallopian tube when the egg is released.

PILLOW *talk*

Another make a baby tip? The woman should have an orgasm. While female orgasm is not a necessary component of conception, there is evidence that uterine contractions that occur during orgasm help sperm move through the fallopian tubes so they can hook up with the egg.

*Civilized people cannot **fully** satisfy their sexual instinct without **love**.*

—Bertrand Russell

Sexological bodyworkers put forth the idea that erotic education and sexual health are basic human rights.

While still on the sketchy list of the helping professions, sexological bodywork is a growing field. Somatic, erotic educators, these trained and certified bodyworkers mainly assist individuals, couples, and groups in how to deepen their experience of embodiment. Sexological bodywork is a new branch of yoga where the practitioners explore how extensively humans learn sex. The practice is embedded in the belief that profound embodied learning takes place only when we repeat a practice mindfully over time.

Sexological bodywork is based on the work of Wilhelm Reich, a respected analyst and controversial figure who did most of his work in the 1940s. Fascinated by energy and sex, his devotion to a device he invented called an Orgone Box landed him a criminal contempt

PILLOW *talk*

Sex is a **natural** *function. You can't make it happen, but you can teach people to* **let it happen**.

—Dr. William H. Masters

charge in court that got him thrown in jail, where he died of heart failure just as he was about to apply for parole. Sexological bodyworkers principally work with those who are psychically ill in that they need only one thing and that is complete and repeated genital gratification. Certificate holders do their training at this time in Switzerland and California where there are organized schools of study.

no.
90

That old adage, "Never go to bed mad," is all wrong.

Zoe Peterson and Erick Janssen, two researchers with the Kinsey Institute, recently conducted a study concluding that when you have are having sex, it doesn't matter much if you're in a good mood or not. What does matter, it turns out, is that you have feelings at all for your partner. It doesn't make much difference whether you love your partner or absolutely hate him. Either way, you'll still have hot sex. It is the absence of emotion—indifference—that causes low response and lack of arousal.

The researchers determined that feeling nothing, or being bored, is the same as emotional avoidance and is related to sexual dysfunction. "For sexual response to occur, it's important to have some emotional reaction," Janssen said.

The study suggests that a combination of emotions may have a distinct impact on sexual functioning and response. "The next step might

PILLOW *talk*

The war between the sexes is the only one in which both sides **regularly** *sleep with the enemy.*

–Quentin Crisp

be to look at how specific combinations of negative and positive emotions, like anxiety or depression and serenity and enthusiasm, might influence sexual functioning and response," Peterson said. In other words, it's not so bad to fight and fuck, and that old adage, "Never go to bed mad," is all wrong. As many people already know, make-up sex after an argument is some of the best sex around!

To get a guy to come, the secret is to stimulate his prostate.

This will automatically trigger a squirt! This practice of "prostate massage" is cool and just the tiniest bit kinky. How to do it? Tell your partner you're going to play with his anus. You might have to try a few positions to find the right access.

Start with him on his back. His knees must be up. Making sure you have no sharp nails that could hurt him, gently insert one lubed finger in about an inch or so. When he's comfortable with the sensation, begin moving upward. Follow the wall of the rectal lining facing the front of his body. When you hit a round bulb of tissue, stop. This is the prostate.

Once you've found the magic bump, move your fingers in a "come here," motion as though you were asking him to come closer so you can tell him a dirty secret. Using the finger pad on the tip of your finger to massage the prostate, keep on massaging and ask him how it feels.

PILLOW *talk*

Healthy, lusty sex is wonderful.

—John Wayne

Let his verbal directive be your guide. It's an enhancement to perform a bit of oral sex or French kissing on him while this is going on. Keep up your rhythm and he's sure to quickly come. If you want to prolong the experience (and ratchet up his pleasure), use a combination move of advancing and retreating, tease your finger on and off the spot until he just can't take it. Remember, you're in control!

92

A Brazilian bikini wax can make you feel hot—or turned off!

A Brazilian bikini wax can make you feel hotter and sexier at least for a day or two because your skin is so sensitive and slightly inflamed from the wax job, and that's erotic. Increased blood flow to the area may make you want to make love . . . or it may make you oversensitive and not able to be touched. In that case, just let your lover stare at your newly bared pubes, salivating. Many guys find a newly naked pussy very stimulating. Don't be surprised if he offers to apply a soothing combination of ice cubes and his wet tongue to all your hot spots. See if that doesn't make you horny!

PILLOW talk

You know [what] they say about a woman being responsible for her own orgasms? That's all true. And in my case, that makes me responsible for pretty damned good orgasms these days. Much better orgasms than when I was twenty-two.

—Halle Berry

no.
93

When presented with sexy pictures, men are more likely to focus on a woman's face and women focus less on faces than body parts!

Dr. Heather Rupp is a leading author who analyzes the viewing patterns of men and women looking at sexual photographs. New material she's recently published in the *Kinsey Institute Journal* reveals the results of that study, which are definitely not what you might think.

Researchers who studied the different ways men and women approached pornography hypothesized that women would look at faces in the photographs and men would look at genitals. Wrong! Instead, they discovered that it's men who are more likely to look at a woman's face and that women focus less on faces than particular body parts! An even bigger surprise was that it turns out women look longer than do men at pictures of men performing sexual acts with women.

PILLOW talk

*If your sexual fantasies were **truly** of interest to others, they would no longer be fantasies.*

—Fran Lebowitz

The study also confirmed that men and women looking at the same sexual material show different patterns of brain activity. "Men looked at the female face much more than women, and both looked at the genitals comparably," said Dr. Rupp. The data also suggested that women's responses varied according to their hormonal state, with women on oral contraceptives paying more attention to genitals than other women in the study.

Drug company competition is fierce for the first to produce feminine Viagra.

While there are many "natural" drug products sold in health food stores and on the web claiming to be as effective for ladies as Viagra is for guys, female sexual dysfunction, that is, lack of libido and little or no lubrication, is more closely connected to how a woman feels about her partner than any physical complaint. Sex for women begins not at the genitals but between the ears. Other conditions, such as hypertension, diabetes, neurological conditions, cancer, and autoimmune diseases wreak havoc on the libido, as do many over-the-counter medications as well as prescription medicines used to treat anxiety and depression.

Women who borrow their husband's Viagra say it increases blood flow to the genitals and blood flow increases lubrication. That said, competition is fierce for which drug company will be the first to produce the a true feminine Viagra. Since 43 percent of women suffer from

PILLOW *talk*

*Among men,
sex sometimes
results in
intimacy;
among women,
intimacy
sometimes
results in sex.*

—Barbara Cartland

sexual dysfunction, as compared to 31 percent of men, it's expected that between $2 and $3 billion will be spent over the next decade developing products directly marketed at improving women's sex lives.

95

Breast implants can decrease—and increase—sensitivity!

Having breast surgery definitely can affect sensitivity, although the changes are usually temporary. And here's a plus to going under the knife: After breast surgery, the nipples may permanently become more sensitive, a side effect most women think is pretty nice.

Newer surgical techniques that do not cut the nerves connected to the nipple increase the chances that a woman will not notice any reduction in sensitivity following her breast augmentation procedure. During surgery, the doctor should avoid interference with the fourth intercostals, one of the nerve branches, that extends to the nipple. This can be accomplished if the implant desired is not too large. If the implant is very large, however, what happens is that the nerve supply gets stretched, and that negatively affects sensitivity.

PILLOW *talk*

The difference between pornography and erotica is *lighting*.

—Gloria Leonard

Plastic surgeons commonly do a test for sensitivity before any cutting happens. The test could be an energy-based stimulation of the nipple or just brushing the nipples with a cotton ball. A common problem that can arise after surgery is capsular contracture, which is when the scar or area around the implant tightens, making the breast feel hard. Nipple desensitivity may follow, although this usually passes after a few weeks. Other causes for breast insensitivity not related to cosmetic surgery are aging skin and thinning skin. Breast cancer diminishes sensitivity too.

no.

96

The latest gadget on everyone's sex toy list lets you stimulate your partner discreetly, in public!

No, it's not the Rabbit or the Pocket Rocket or even the Fukuoku 9000 Finger Vibe, although those are all top sellers at online sex toy stores. No, the most coveted object is a toy two can play with together, even in public (especially in public!) — remote control vibrating panties. What is that, you ask? Panties (or pants . . . they make 'em for men and for women) with a tiny vibrator sewn into the crotch that can be activated from a distance of up to twelve feet by the person holding the remote. Bzzzzz! You've been zapped!

Promoted by Dr. Laura Berman on her Showtime program *Sexual Healing*, these novelty panties are a lot of fun. Part of the thrill is that the pants create an immediate dominant/submissive (but playful) relationship. The person holding the remote has all the control. He can arouse his partner at will and she is but a helpless puppet vibrating to his command.

Sex is God's

joke

on human beings.

–Bette Davis

When a woman licks her lips, it means she is horny.

In fact, she might be so horny she has no control over her involuntary gestures, like her mouth going all dry at the very sight of you. Or she may be licking her lips deliberately, twisting her mouth into a big O and then running her tongue all around it in circles to show you what she intends her tongue and lips to do to your cock. For a less openly sexual girl, the lip licking could also just mean that she's very attracted to you, that she finds you a hot and sexy heartthrob. Or it could mean that she's a little nervous, that she's a bit discomfited by you, that your presence makes her jumpy and has turned her dry-mouthed. In fact, she could use a glass of water. Dry mouth, incidentally, is a sign of sexual tension, a body language thing where the body tells the mind there's something going on here.

Body language aside, there is quite a difference, however, between a deliberate lip lick and the lick that is subconscious. A deliberate lick, such as the woman who has a long, wide, flat, carpet of a tongue who lets it wander enticingly in a circle over her slightly parted, oval shaped lips, is playfully telling you she's very oral and hungry for you.

The flip side is the female who can't stop biting her lip in your presence or whose tongue nervously darts out of her mouth to moisten her lips while you're speaking to her or looking straight at her is jonesing for you, but she doesn't seem all that happy to be around you. What's that about? It means she doesn't know if you feel the same way about her, or if one of you should make a move, or if you happen to be her boss, how she can cover up her desire in a way that won't embarrass her. In any case, lip licking is a sign of anxiousness and sexual desire. Proceed accordingly.

PILLOW talk

You know that look women get when they want sex? Me neither.

—Drew Carey, American comedian

98

The only purpose of the clitoris is to give the woman sexual pleasure.

The clitoris, labia, urethra, and opening to the vagina are all part of what is known as the vulva. The tip of the clitoris is what's visible to the eye; it may be smaller than a pea or bigger than a fingertip, depending on the build of the woman. (Taking steroids, by the way, if you happen to be an athlete, will make your clitoris larger.) The tip of the clitoris can be seen at the top of the vulva in the soft folds of the labia. The rest of the clitoris is inside the body and can be up to five inches long. Just as the tip may be large or small, every woman's full clitoris is slightly differently sized and has different levels of sensitivity. The only purpose of the clitoris is to give the woman sexual pleasure. There is no reproductive function.

If you're pleasuring a woman with your finger or your tongue, ask her how she prefers to have her clit stimulated. Some women enjoy direct contact; for others, that's too intense. If she's very sensitive, try massaging the area on either side of her clit to lubricate and arouse her. Hint: massage to the right if she's a righty, the left if she's a lefty. That is how she most likely masturbates and the way she's trained her body to respond to touch. Why mess around? Have her show you her clit and then ask her to demonstrate or describe the way she wants it touched.

PILLOW *talk*

Sex is **hardly** *ever* *just about sex.*

—Shirley MacLaine

Thanks to modern technology just about anyone (over eighteen) can engage in group sex . . . without ever leaving the house.

It used to be that if you were planning on participating in an orgy, you had to actually get up and go somewhere. Enter the wide world of the webcam. By simply hooking multiple screens up on your desktop computer, you can have a big ol' masturbation party right in the comfort of your home. It's certainly one way to have the kind of wild and crazy sexual encounters you'd never actually dare in the flesh.

PILLOW *talk*

The good thing about masturbation is that you don't have to dress up for it.

—Truman Capote

It's called "screwing" for a reason!

When you screw, you move in a circular motion, you don't hammer it straight in. Guys who get it about screwing are always in demand. How to do it? Place the penis deep inside the vagina, but instead of thrusting in and out, grind the hips in a spiral fashion, like a screw, and you'll hit all the hidden parts. The clitoris is more than just the tip. All around the top and bottom and the sides are pleasure-loving nerve endings that can only be touched by this movement. These hidden parts are believed to account for 90 percent of female sensations, so you don't want to miss those parts! Still want to hit the tip? Push your hips up a notch at the tightest point of the screwing motion. See if that doesn't produce multiple orgasms!

PILLOW
talk

It is essential that we realize once and for all that man is much more of a sex creature than a moral creature.

—Emma Goldman

101

Contrary to popular opinion, the most erogenous zone on a woman is *not* between her legs.

It's definitely not the clit, which *becomes* the most erogenous zone, but only after her other erogenous zones have been alerted. It's not her nipples either, although they respond nicely to being lightly pinched and sucked. There's an entire system of nerves connecting the groin to the breasts and nipples which is why so many women love having their breasts stimulated during foreplay and absolutely when they're having sex. But the breasts and the nipples are not the most erogenous zones.

Eastern Indians and students of the Kama Sutra maintain the most sensitive place on a woman's body is the back of her neck and her ear lobes. That's why the Kama Sutra, the ancient, most famous and renowned book of love, suggests first caressing a woman on the back of her neck. The book advises covering a woman's neck with soft, hot kisses and nibbling at her ear lobes. In most Eastern cultures an erotic gift to a woman is a pair of dangly chandelier earrings. The weight of the earrings gently tugs at her lobes, simulating the way his lips would do the same thing. Plus the length of the earrings causes them to brush gently against her neck, another erotic stimulation. Such earrings are a love offering or token meant to keep the woman in a constant state of low-level excitement in preparation for the caress of her lover.

The back of a woman's neck is indeed very sensitive and many women say it is their most erogenous zone. In fact, the entire surface of all skin is erogenous, which is the reason why so many highly sensitive women adore being tickled. For them, being tickled is a form of sex. Many researchers, however, believe that the most erogenous zone a woman has is between her ears. It's the brain. If you stimulate a woman mentally, she's absolutely going to find you very arousing.

PILLOW
talk

Everyone probably thinks that I'm a raving nymphomaniac, that I have an insatiable sexual appetite, when the truth is I'd rather read a book.

—Madonna

About the Author

Eve Marx, MA is a bona fide sexpert. She's published a number of books on relationships and sex including *Read My Hips*, *What's Your Sexual IQ?*, *The Goddess Orgasm*, and, most recently, *Flirtspeak: The Sexy Guide to Flirting*. She is a former editor of *Penthouse Forum* and *Swank* magazine, as well as a contributor to *Cosmopolitan*, *Savvy Miss*, and *Men's Health*. Visit her website at *www.evemarx.com*, or read her blog at *www.evemarx.blogspot.com*. She lives in Katonah, New York.